Having My Say

Conversations With
Chesapeake Bay Waterman
Wylie "Gator" Abbott

Other Books Co-Authored By A. M. Foley

Elliott's Island: The Land That Time Forgot

Cambridge: A Pictorial History

Dorchester County: A Pictorial History

Having My Say
Conversations With
Chesapeake Bay Waterman
Wylie "Gator" Abbott

By A.M. Foley

Dogwood Ridge Books – Elliott Island, Maryland

Book Design by Jim Slattery
Ann Slattery, Editor
Cover Design by Kathleen Barnes
Cover Photo by Francis I. duPont

Portions have appeared previously in
Elliott's Island: The Land That Time Forgot
Available from this publisher
For information or additional copies contact:
Dogwood Ridge Books
2336 Elliott Island Road
Elliott Island, MD 21869
dogwdbooks@shorenet.net

Library of Congress Control Number 2005908961
ISBN 10: 0-9672947-2-X
ISBN 13: 978-0-9672947-2-8

Printed in the United States of America

The Dorchester Marshes

. . . where the sky meets the bayou and man's eye can search only the marsh grass waving in the spring like a sea of green, in the fall like a mammoth field of wheat waiting for the harvest. God was not slow to inhabit these bayous with some of the finest muskrat trappers in the world.

Elihu Abbott, *The Daily Banner*, 1969

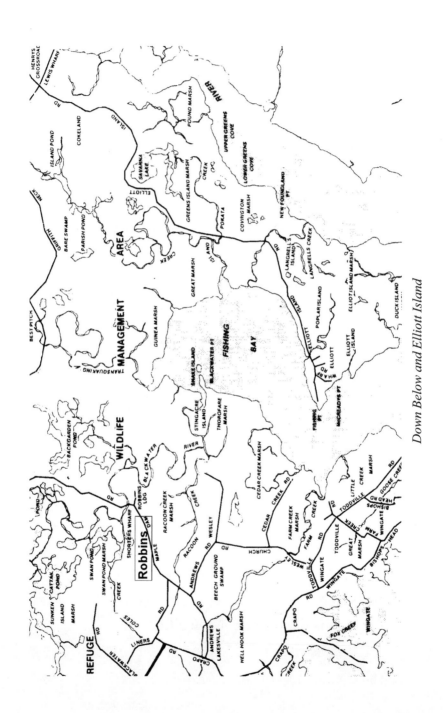

Down Below and Elliott Island

Contents

*A*cknowledgements

So many took an interest in the success of our effort, an alphabetical approach seems the only way to say thanks. The author is most grateful for help received from Doris Abbott, Teresa Abbott, Pamela and Wylie Abbott Jr., Harold Dean Brittingham, Tim Cashman, Chip Chew, Francis I. duPont, Michael Foley, Geoffrey Footner, Jan and Steve Gray, Marie and Phillip Gray, James Jackson, Thomas Jackson, Gloria Johnson, Abby Katze, Joe Lemen, Beverly Lynch, Debby Moxey and her *Dorchester County Genealogy Magazine*, Ann Slattery, Brice Stump, Paul Tillman, Freddie Waller, Mary Ellen and Waner Waller, and Wendy Abbott White.

Some images were published previously in *The Daily Banner* and are reprinted with the kind permission of its editor, Dave Ryan. Small portions appeared earlier from interviews done for *Elliott's Island: The Land That Time Forgot*, written with Freddie T. Waller and published by Dogwood Ridge Books. Some photographs were taken by the late Jennie and Joe Norton, whose collection has been preserved by Freida and Ed Gray.

This work achieved its present form due to the artistic and electronic wizardry of others, most notable Kathleen Barnes; Gary Thompson and Mike Munion of Hurst Creek Computers; Katie Slattery Lemen; and most especially, Jim Slattery.

A. M. F.

£isting of Photographs

*A*uthor's *N*ote

When I first left Cabin John for Elliott Island, I had difficulty following conversations in this far more amphibious part of Maryland. As my friend Eva Thomas said, "Around the Island here, near about every tree has a name." Wylie Abbott was one of the Islanders who translated place names and nicknames into terms I understood, and explained how watery things worked in general. I'm grateful to him and his kind for their patience with me.

I had the good luck to listen to his adventures for twenty-odd years, more often than not in Nora Foxwell's store. In the last year of his life, whenever he had nothing more interesting going on, he submitted to interviews. Wylie died, darn it, before anything came of it, but this book is the result, his story assembled and retold as faithfully as I can get it on paper. Should any inaccuracies have crept in, they're most probably mine.

I only wish I could write as well as Wylie could talk.

A. M. Foley
Elliott Island, Maryland

$\mathcal{P}$rologue

"GATOR"

Elliott Island Harbor, October 2004

Some years ago, an old boy from Robbins, Maryland named Merritt Robbins was traveling near a river down in Virginia. Some Abbotts, cousins of my father, had moved there and Merritt thought he'd look them up. When he got to the little section they lived into, he stopped to ask a man directions.

Merritt said, I'm lookin' for some Abbotts who used to be neighbors of mine in Maryland. They work on the water 'round here.

The man said, Yeah, sure. I know them Abbotts. They're a fine bunch of people, but the biggest liars you'll ever meet.

Yeah, said Merritt, that's just who I'm lookin' for.

***

People can judge for themselves how fine a person this Abbott is, but if I tell a lie here, it'll be an accident.

– Wylie M. Abbott, Sr. (1940-2005)

Chapter 1

I was born January 16, 1940. The weekend my mother brought me from the hospital, it snowed so deep they had to hook oxen onto our car to pull us the last five miles to her mother's house at Shorters Wharf. Later in life, one of my uncles used to tease me every time he got drunk.

Wylie, he'd say, damn you're a hard case. You're lucky to be livin' today. When you were born, I drug through snow knee-deep to get you home in a blizzard. I saved your life that night. Get me a six-pack up the road when you go.

What happened was, they wanted me home so bad that a whole carful of my mother's people drove to Cambridge in a snowstorm to get us from the hospital. Before they reached back home with us, the old car stuck in a drift. The Handley family farmed on Maple Dam Road and kept a pair of oxen, so my uncle walked up to their place. Mr. Handley came down with his oxen and latched them onto us. Oxen are so slow, lord only knows what time we finally got to my grandmother's house, but oxen can plow through any snowbank. They drug us down Maple Dam Road, across the bridge to Shorters Wharf, and up the lane to my grandmother Robbins' house.

At first they named me after the doctor who delivered me, Dr. Wylie Faw, but somebody got a notion to change my middle name and I became Wylie Marvin Abbott. I grew up in Dorchester County, Maryland at Robbins with my two brothers. Jimmy was a year and two days younger than me and Doug was a year and a half younger than Jimmy. Except for Jimmy being overseas in the Army, none of us ever moved far from Robbins. I moved the farthest—across Fishing Bay to Elliotts Island—six miles as the crow flies. Without wings, it takes nearly an hour by car, on roads winding through marshes and over more rivers, creeks, and guts than you can count. Me and Jimmy worked just about all our lives on that water or in all that marsh around there. Doug did too, off and on, but he ended up on land, working for Cambridge Wire Cloth.

***

I was three years old when our father, Winnie Abbott, went away to the army, drafted at thirty-eight into World War II, leaving behind us three boys and our mother, Dorothy Robbins Abbott. I can't hardly remember Daddy before he left, but I know he was building a house for us at the time, or rebuilding it. A good-sized house had been for sale along the road in Robbins, a couple miles inland from Shorters Wharf. Daddy bought half of it and Mace Robbins bought the rest. They cut the house in two and Daddy had his half drug down the road on skids. He just did get her back across the ditch-bank and set up on a foundation before he got called into the Army.

Winnie and Dorothy Abbott

One whole side of our house was still open, where they'd cut her half-in-two. Daddy fastened that side up with sailcloth or something, so we could stay in there till he got back. I remember seeing the stars through the crack at night and watching snow fall. We stayed there like that till he came back from Europe. He was gone for over two years.

***

Daddy must have rigged up the oil burner before he left, 'cause I don't remember carrying wood. Many a bucket of water got toted, though. Back on Mace Robbins' place, where our house came from, Mace had a deep well.

Mom would say, Come on, boys. Wylie, get the wagon.

We had a little wagon and a couple of ten-gallon milk cans. She herded us boys up and down the road to Mace's, pulling the wagon for water, till finally the war ended.

Mom was a pretty woman with jet-black hair. One day she got all fixed up, putting on her good dress and lipstick.

She said, You boys stay with Mamma Robbins while we go to Cambridge and collect your Daddy from the bus station.

I'm sure I couldn't have picked Daddy out in a bus station, especially among all the men in uniform then. When Mom finally came home with him, he carried a big duffel bag with presents from Germany. He wasn't much

Winnie Abbott

taller than Mom and his hair had turned frosty-looking—gray hair mixed with dark. His feet had gotten frostbitten and he walked a little tender, but he wasn't long getting back to work.

Daddy built the fourth wall onto the house, then had a well drilled on our place. My mother's brother, Campbell Robbins, lived alongside of us, so what he and Daddy did was, they had a well drilled and went fifty-fifty on one pump for the two houses. It worked like that for many a year, but I don't guess the government would let you do that now.

Mom's brother Campbell was a preacher. Their father, James Wesley Robbins, died before I was born. Cap'n Jim, he was called. Their mother was Cap'n Jim's second wife, Minnie Robbins. who lived just up the road from us on the Blackwater River at Shorters Wharf. We boys stayed up there a lot, especially me.

Chapter 2

THE ABBOTTS

I didn't know neither grandfather. I'm told Daddy's father, George W. Abbott, sailed up from Deals Island and anchored down at Robbins Landing after getting hung up with my grandmother. Granddad Abbott must have already had uncles or cousins around Robbins, or else brought some with him. Abbotts were as thick as mosquitoes around Robbins. Old-timers said they liked listening to my grandfather, that he was a nice-talking man.

Nobody never did work much on family trees till late years. Nobody said much about ancestors when I was a youngster, but we knew we had a lot of Indian. Supposedly I had a great-grandfather who was a chief on my Abbott side. The Robbins side might have had some Indian too, but not as much.

Daddy's mother, Lola Hurley Abbott, lived by the Blackwater River just like Mom's mother did, only at Robbins Landing, a few miles down river from Shorters Wharf. By land from our place, Mamma Abbott's house was about three miles—way back through the woods.

Some claim Robbins Landing is haunted with ghost lights, but any lights I saw around there, I think were just marsh gas. I'm sure no ghost lights ever scared Mamma Abbott. She may have been just a little thing, but nothing scared her. If Indians lived around there still, they looked like her. She was outdoors a lot, dark complected, with dark hair she always wore in a ponytail. She wasn't wrinkled, even at seventy. She looked good.

***

Going up Blackwater River from Fishing Bay, you'll never find Robbins Landing if you don't know what to look for. You come to it three or four miles before Shorters Wharf Bridge—bare marsh just like everywhere else along the river,

Lola Hurley Abbott and George W. Abbott photographed at Robbins Landing with daughter Helen around 1930, four years before George's death

only it's hard bottom. About a mile across that hard-bottom marsh, you see the woods where my grandmother lived.

Daddy walked us back there sometimes for weekends when he and Mom wanted to take off someplace. To get there on foot from our house, we had to walk up the road towards Shorters Wharf about a mile and a half, to a path going off into some woods. About a mile down along that path, we came to a pond—probably fifty feet wide. We had to cross on a bridge made of great big logs split in two, fastened on poles driven down into the pond bottom. This bridge wasn't two feet wide, with no railing or nothing. After getting a little age on us, we boys had a big time horsing around on that bridge, making like we were gonna push each other off or falling in the pond. But I remember being scared the first time Daddy took us back in there. The woods were thick and dark and tidal pools and mud smelled strong and briny.

***

Mamma Abbott crossed that bridge many a time. In her day they walked and toted everything they used. When the sheep flies hit or the mosquitoes buzzed, that was some walk, especially if your hands were taken up with toting something.

She raised ten young'uns back there on the high ground between the pond and the river, where she had a regular two-story house. We called it Robbins Landing or Back Landing. Another name for grandmother's place was Pine Landing. Some nice pine trees stood there before Hurricane Hazel, but they got blown down. I'm told four houses stood there at one time, but I only saw Mamma Abbott's house. She had a smokehouse out back, where she hung meat she'd smoked outside over a fire. She had a privy, of course. At one time they must have kept a horse or two, because there was an old stable, but in our time she just kept a dog and a couple cats. Outside there were a few chickens and sometimes a hog in a pen.

***

When we went back to stay over with her, we played around in the ponds or the marsh, then at a certain time Mamma called, Come on, boys. Suppertime.

More often than not, we trooped in wet and muddy. After we washed up and ate supper, she put us to bed upstairs, three in a bed. Even from upstairs, we couldn't see another house or any light on land, but sometimes boat lights ran up and down Blackwater River.

If Mamma heard us from downstairs, she called to us, You boys quiet down and go to sleep up there.

Once we climbed in that bed, she didn't allow no cutting up, the way three little boys can do. We quieted down and fell asleep, listening to a night bird or boat engine. Then in the morning we smelled breakfast cooking downstairs. We went down and found her cooking at this big wood-burning stove—an old-time breakfast of eggs, bacon, scrapple, and biscuits. She had plenty to eat back there, but you couldn't drive a well by that marsh. She had to have her sons help tote all her water back to her. Her lamps lit with kerosene, so they had to tote that too.

***

A widow-woman, Nellie Willey, lived with her. Nellie couldn't do much of nothing in the time we knew her, so Mamma did for her too. Nellie was the widow of Mack Willey, who's been called The Cow-man of Robbins. In that part of the county—what's called Down Below—cows used to be turned loose to graze. It's been said Mack Willey stayed out in the marsh with the cows and grew up wild, but I don't think he grew up any wilder than the rest of them. Maybe he stayed some nights out there on the marsh with the cows, suckling and eating marsh grass like people said. They claimed he was the son of a witch who lived at Bestpitch Ferry.

I just did miss knowing him, but I remember hearing how old Mack Willey used to keep folks around Robbins in an uproar about all the ghost lights he saw.

Daddy's sister, my Aunt Helen, said some of those noises Mack thought were hauntings were just the boys playing tricks on him and Nellie.

After Mack settled down with Nellie, they had their own little house—one of the four houses old-timers remembered back there at Robbins Landing. Mack kept a pair of oxen and cut and sold firewood. Mack and Nellie are the only other ones I know of besides Daddy's family to live at the landing, so I don't know who lived in the other two houses.

***

I don't see how they survived winters. Of course, they got everything up before the weather turned cold. That's all they did do—get stuff up to live off of. Mamma got her wood up for her stove and got her meats salted down and hung in her smokehouse. She had a little hill high enough for a garden and she put up beans and peas and tomatoes and banked potatoes in the ground. She hunted small game—kept little rabbit 'gums,' which worked like live-boxes used for trapping. She set gums up on sticks all around the edge of the yard. When a rabbit or squirrel went in to get the bait, it tripped the gum. Mamma caught possums, too, and ate them, but I never did.

In the old days, hogs roamed loose anywhere, just like cows did. Some didn't belong to anybody. At a certain time of year they penned and fattened the hogs up.

Later, I had an Elliotts Island neighbor, Dick Shorter, who'd been born down below in Cains Ditch. Dick was about twenty years older than me. After I moved to the Island, on rainy days or when it was blowing bad, we used to sit around in Nora Foxwell's store.

Dick said of his dad, In my father's time, they kept special hog dogs they took out in the woods when they wanted meat. Those hog dogs would grab a wild hog somewhere in the back of the leg so that it couldn't move.

I don't remember any wild hogs or hog dogs in my time. I just remember the hog being in the pen. And I remember when they had a hog-killing, Mamma used it all. Nothing got thrown away. I helped her clean up intestines that she put up in quart jars. I wouldn't eat chitterlings from a store, but I liked them when Mamma fixed them. When they got the hog down to the fat, Mamma made lye soap.

Chapter 3

CANNERIES

Back in those days everybody worked, I don't care how small they were. Three canning houses packed tomatoes around home in the 1940s. Anybody with enough high land grew a tomato patch. When she wasn't picking crabs in the summer, Mom skinned tomatoes at Leonard's cannery on Blackwater River or at Baker Robbins' in Andrews. In August, whole families would be in the tomato patches, going down rows with baskets. Before Daddy got back to his regular work, he took us picking tomatoes. We boys couldn't carry baskets yet, that's how small we were.

Daddy gave us each a one-gallon paint can to pick into and put a peck basket about fifty feet down the row ahead of us.

Here, boys, he said, when your can gets full, empty it into that basket.

Bigger kids and their parents and grandparents worked their way on down their rows. We three boys straggled along, holding our bucket handles and dumping tomatoes into the basket when the can got heavy. We thought we were doing something.

***

The tomato cannery wasn't as safe as a crabhouse. The cannery had lots of machinery and conveyers with moving belts. We were too small for any work in there, but Mom had to take us along when Daddy got a job at his regular work, boatbuilding at the Oxford shipyard.

It was still dark outside the cannery when we got off the bus that rounded up the workers. Mom had a regular place to sit at a worktable skinning tomatoes. Before she started, she turned three baskets over behind her stool.

You boys sit down, she said. Behave yourselves there till I say you can go.

We three sat there on those baskets till daylight. She had her hands full keeping us boys still for a couple hours, but no three little fellas could be running around in such a loud, busy place. We watched as a merry-go-round carried buckets with the skinners' numbers written on their sides. When Mom's bucket came around, she saw it was hers and picked it off. When she had it filled, she sent it on around to a man who dumped it in the canning machine. She got paid by the bucket.

When the sun got up good, then she turned us loose. We were everywhere around the ditches outside the cannery. We made fishing hooks out of nails. We filed them sharp, bent them over, and tied them on string, then baited with

Dorothy Robbins Abbott with Doug, Jimmy, and Wylie

tomato cores. A big pipe ran the skins from the cannery to the river. We'd sit on the pipe fishing with our handlines. Carp came up and grabbed on the nails to get the tomato chunks.

One day Jimmy started hollering, Help, it's a big one...I'm goin' overboard!

The way that tomato waste smelled, nobody wanted to go in that water. Me and Doug grabbed onto Jimmy and pulled. It took all three of us holding onto the old drain pipe and pulling, but we landed that carp.

We ran inside with it all excited saying, Look what we caught!

Mom took us out to the big scales on the landing platform and had it weighed for us. The man there laid the carp on the tomato-weighing scales and started fiddling with the weights.

Getting it in balance, he said, I'll be darn. A twenty-six pound carp. You boys are all right.

***

An old woman bought carp from us for 25-cents a fish. Every day around dinnertime, she came back to the cannery selling fish sandwiches for 25-cents apiece. She sold other things too, but fish sandwiches were her top dinner. She didn't call them carp; she called them steak sandwiches. Most days she gave each of us boys a free sandwich. They were really good.

In a creek across from our house, Snare Pole Gut, we caught white perch. We could sell a string of five or six perch for a quarter to workers at the canning house. We thought that was big money, till Jimmy one day went into an old barn alongside the canning house and came out with a swallow's nest made of mud, with a dollar bill worked into it. I don't know what ever happened to that nest, but we never spent that dollar bill. Mom kept it a lot of years for us. I'd like to have it now.

***

When Mom picked crabs, we went there with her too, riding the bus sent around before daylight to gather everybody up. In the beginning, we were so little, when we got to the crabhouse, Mom put us in empty crab-can boxes to sleep awhile. Around seven or eight o'clock, she woke us and we got up and cracked claws for a while. They paid us 15-cents a pound, same as the grown-up claw-crackers. I learned to pick a crab, too. I got so good in time, I bet I could pick thirty or thirty-five pounds a day.

Mom picked for George Powley's in Wingate, and wintertimes she shucked oysters there. In January and February, whenever we weren't in school, we fooled around with our father hunting traps—muskrating. We'd walk his marsh with him, or set our own traps along the road.

Chapter 4

OUR WORLD

Little one-room schoolhouses stood scattered all over down below, near enough that everybody could walk to one or another of them. The Robbins School stood near enough, I could have thrown a baseball from our house and hit it. It went up to seventh grade. Fifteen or twenty of us went there—about half either Robbins or Abbott. Our cousins Theodore and Elihu Abbott lived in Robbins. Theodore was in the same grade with me. His brother Elihu, ten years older, graduated before we started.

We had three or four different teachers while in that school. One I remember was a Todd from Toddville, a little old man with glasses who wore garters on the sleeves of his shirt, up by his elbows. When he was younger, he taught on Elliotts Island, sailing back and forth every day. When Fishing Bay froze up, he ice-skated over to the Island.

When Dougie got old enough, me and Jimmy took him along to school with us. Before long, Dougie brought his first report card home to Mom.

She looked at it and said, It's all Es, Dougie! What are you doing? You've got to learn.

He said, Mom, I'm playing just as hard as I can!

I guess me and Jimmy weren't very good examples for Dougie, but I can't remember us getting in much trouble in Robbins School. For a little bit of nothing, I had to hold my palms up one time for Mr. Todd to smack, but I never got my bottom paddled before I got to high school.

***

One boy a little older than me who went to school with us, George Andrews, lived in Andrews and came from Wesley Road on a bicycle, the onliest bicycle at Robbins School. It looked like a regular bike, only it had a little motor on it called a Wizard. He could go about twenty-five miles-an-hour. We'd put seven or eight boys on her, on the handlebars and fenders and everywhere. One day I climbed aboard last and held on to the next-to-last boy. We hit a bump and I slid off the back and skinned my backside, ripping my britches. It happened right there by the school. I went home and my mother liked to give me a thrashing, even before she saw my britches.

What are you doing out of school at this time of day? she wanted to know.

I told her what happened and showed her my britches.

You go change and get back to school, she said.

She patched my school britches while I went back to school in my other pair. They did a lot of patching and darning in those days.

***

A couple years after Daddy came home from the war, he bought a blue International Carry-All from Meredith and Meredith, at the foot of the bridge in Cambridge. Six or eight boatbuilders from down below rode with him to work at the Oxford shipyard.

Less than a mile from the Robbins School was our church, Bounds Methodist, a pretty little country church. By the time we boys got old enough for Sunday School, Daddy had the Carry-All. Every Sunday morning, Mom scrubbed us up and drove us to church. Grown-ups went mornings and again in the evening for a prayer service at eight o'clock. We had to be pretty good in church in the morning, but played around outside Sunday evenings. I remember us getting a hold of a cigar out there one evening. One boy's father kept his cigar on the doorstep to save it while he went into church.

Sometimes we had special programs inside Bounds, there being no church hall at that time. Every Christmas night

Bounds Church photographed in 2004

our Sunday School gave a program where everybody got up and sang or made a speech. Jerol Moore, my best buddy, was learning the saxophone. For the big holiday program, he studied a song to play along with one of the girls, Judy, at the piano. In my pocket that night, I had some berries from holly bushes that grew in the fields along the road.

When Jerol wasn't looking, I told Jimmy, Watch this.

I slipped a handful of holly berries down Jerol's tube. His mother and father sat back in their pew, just waiting for him to get up there. Judy started on the piano and Jerol locked in on his sax, threw down a big blow, and all he got was a squeal. His face started getting red and you could see the blood vessels coming out on his neck, but the saxophone just kept squealing like a pig. We were all laughing. Jerol didn't care, but boy, his mother was a mad woman.

She said, I'd like to know who done that.

I don't believe she ever figured out whose holly berries they were. For my own job, I had a speech to do—something about the Bible. Somebody made it up for me to give out, just like they do for the President. All three of us boys had speeches, and we sang some in the chorus. They'd never get us to stand up there and sing by ourselves, but we sang in one of the stores down home.

***

An old guy, Jimmy Stewart, had a little store on the road to Toddville. Sometimes Daddy stopped there coming home from tonging oysters.

Mr. Jimmy would tell Daddy, Come back down tonight and bring those boys. I want 'em to sing for me.

We were around five, six, and seven then. Daddy would carry us down. There might be eight or ten men sitting around inside there on benches. If she knew we were coming, maybe Mrs. Virginia Stewart walked over from their house next door.

We'd walk in and Mr. Jimmy would say, Evenin' boys! I got popsicles and candy bars today.

Mr. Jimmy always had certain songs he wanted to hear. We had a job getting started, but once we got going, we could sing pretty good, especially for a nice big popsicle. We sang whatever he wanted—some hillbilly songs we learned—usually something by Hank Williams like 'Cold, Cold Heart,' 'Hey Good Lookin',' or 'Your Cheating Heart.'

When we finished singing, we sat there eating up our candy or popsicle. Mr. Jimmy and others chewed tobacco, so he kept an old five-pound lard can handy. Watching us eat, he'd spit into his spit-can and wipe his hand across his mouth and shake his head.

Looking at the other men, he'd say, Them boys are right, ain't they?

The other men always laughed and asked, Cap'n Jimmy, when are them boys coming back?

***

Another old man called Pop King came by about three times a week in a big old yellow school bus. Grown-ups didn't fool with him much, but kids came running when they saw him coming. You could get on the bus and walk through. He had wooden chicken crates with chickens into them that he sold or swapped along the way. He had a mess of kid stuff that we got—cakes and candy and pop. We dealt him whatever we had: turtle eggs (turkle, we said), or blackberries we picked, or some of the wild 'spargus that grew on Sandy Island and along the ditch-banks. Sometimes we hitched a ride with him from our house as far as Shorters Wharf, where Mamma Robbins lived.

We liked messing around the riverside there—progging it was called. We spent all summer progging in and around the water in cut-off jeans or bathing suits and sneakers. One day we were progging close to home. Dougie and I lost sight of Jimmy. After a little while, we heard him hollering for us.

Hey, guys! Come here! Come here!

We ran towards Mace Robbins', where a ditch ran all around the house, but we didn't find Jimmy.

I said, Where the heck's he at? I can't see him! Jimmy! Over here!

He kept on hollering till finally we found him behind Mace's house, lying flat on the marsh, hanging halfway in the ditch. He'd spotted a 15-inch snapping turkle swimming in there and grabbed its tail. Jimmy hung over the edge of the ditch, one hand holding himself from falling in head-first, the other holding the turkle's tail. If a turkle can get his feet on the ground it can really pull. This one was too big for Jimmy to land by himself, but he wouldn't let go. Me and Doug each grabbed one of Jimmy's legs and started tugging. Between the three of us, we hauled that turkle up.

***

We made good money off turkles, even as little kids. Around May when it warms up, in an ebb-and-flowing pond, when the tide goes out, you can see tracks where a turkle is buried in the mud. If you poke a stick down by his head, he'll grab and hold on. You can pull him right out on the stick. Or you feel down in the mud for his shell, put a hand on his back to tell which way he's headed—feel which way the ridges run so you can slide your hand back and make sure you don't grab the wrong end. We liked to go out after snappers in a thunderstorm. When thunder claps, they pop their heads up.

We rode turkles, too, and it didn't take a real big one. We stood on his shell and he'd raise right up. They're slow, but they'd walk with us. We balanced on their backs with our walking sticks, riding right along. The men all carried walking sticks when they went out in the marsh—thin poles nearly as long as the man was tall. Naturally, if they carried walking sticks, we boys had to carry them too.

***

I wasn't too bad about it, but Jimmy liked to mess with snapping turkles—make them mean and get them snapping at twigs and things. A decent-sized turkle can shoot his neck six inches to grab something. One day we were outside our cousin Theodore's house, Jimmy sitting on the kitchen door-stoop messing around with this big turkle. All of a sudden, the thing shot his head out and set down on the tip of Jimmy's thumb. Jimmy was about twelve, too old to cry, but you could see the tears coming into his eyes.

Help me, he said. Get me loose!

I tried everything to make that snapper let go. I tried pliers, but couldn't budge it. The big old thing had Jimmy anchored right where he sat. Old-timers used to say if a snapper got hold of you, it wouldn't turn loose till thunder sounded.

I remembered another old saying and said, I believe a snapper'll turn loose if you stick a straw up its nose. Where's Aunt Inez's broom?

We found her broom behind the door and I pulled out a straw and tickled up the turkle's nose. He popped his old mouth right open. That's the last snapping turkle Jimmy messed around with. None ever got a hold of me.

***

Before I got teenaged, we were catching so many turkles Daddy rode us to a market with them in his pickup. We stored them in fifty-gallon barrels with lids. Turkles will live a month or more in a barrel, but we boys wanted money. It didn't take very long before we had two or three barrels caught up. Daddy backed his truck up with an empty barrel in the back and we passed turkles up one by one till it was nearly full. When we had two or three barrels loaded like that, we carried them to Jinx Dickson on Washington Street in Cambridge. Mr. Jinx bought anything in the seafood line, fish, muskrats, anything.

We never saved up our money for nothing big. Besides sweets, we bought fishing line or something to crab with, stuff like that.

Chapter 5

SHORTERS WHARF

As soon as me and Jimmy both got old enough to walk, we were everywhere, but especially down to Shorters Wharf. Something was always going on around there, where the bridge carries the road to Cambridge across the Blackwater River. Reese Todd had his boathouse there where he built new boats, and Daddy kept a little railway there, where anybody could pull a boat up for repairs. Mom's mother and some of her brothers and sisters lived there, too. My Aunt Ruth and Reese Todd's daughter Jeanette were good friends and used to make over me. I remember them swinging me on Mr. Reese's porch. I used to have a photo of the three of us in that big porch swing, me a little guy with hair black as smut down to my shoulders. I got that black hair from my mother.

I remember the old low-rise drawbridge over the Blackwater River that pivoted in the middle, so boats could go by on either side. It had a little house halfway across, in the middle of the river, but I can't remember any bridge-tender staying in there. Maybe anybody who happened to be around opened the bridge. Not even a skiff could pass without somebody turning the wheel to the crank that swung the draw around. Later the county built a bridge high enough for boats to go underneath.

On our end of the bridge, Reese Todd's boathouse stood on one side of the road and his dwelling house, where we used to swing, stood on the other. Right behind Reese Todd's stood Mamma Robbins'—a two-story frame house with porches. She was an able lady, a little taller and huskier than Daddy's mother, with grey hair. She wore her hair shorter than Mamma Abbott's. She had plenty of daughters around, so they probably kept her more up-to-date in style.

Boy, Mamma Robbins could cook a dinner. She kept a big, wood-burning cookstove fired up in the kitchen. Every Sunday, she had twenty or thirty people there eating dinner. That was *every* Sunday. She baked three or four cakes and pies. When it froze up in the winter, she got one of her boys to chop ice out of the river to pack down into the ice cream-maker for cranking vanilla or chocolate ice cream. Afterwards, we got the paddles to lick. Even her grown-up kids, like Dave and Joe and Ruth, liked to lick the paddles. I don't remember us boys ever fighting over them. Sometimes I might be the onliest one there and I'd get it all.

Mamma had a good-sized kitchen with two kerosene lamps hanging down for light and a bunch of chairs set around the room to be pulled up to the table at dinnertime. Others sat eating on the porch. She had a big table on the back porch where she kept her sweets she baked on weekends, sometimes chocolate or coconut pie, sweet potato pie, coconut or chocolate cake. You couldn't put on a dinner now like she did; it'd cost you $500. She had lots of seafood: rockfish, oyster, crab, snapping turkle. A snapper has seven different kinds of meat in him. She made something different with it every Sunday—wouldn't be the same thing. She cleaned the turkle: cut the shell off, took out the meat, and made stew or snapper soup.

There was no such thing then as single-fried oysters, just flitters. (We never said 'fritter' down below.) Mamma could make an oyster flitter—and a crab cake. Up the road everybody wants crab cakes big and they're full of batter. She made them small, all meat, and delicious.

Sometimes me and Jimmy would bring her a big carp. She skinned and soaked them overnight in salt water. Carp was something good to eat when she got through with it. After we got older, big rockfish weren't legal, but if we carried her one of those thirty- or forty- pounders, she went out in the shed and got her hoe to scale it. She cooked for everybody who came around till she wasn't able to do it no more.

***

Like everybody else who lived around there, my grandmother had a privy hanging overboard. Before we were big enough to fool around the riverbank fishing, we three boys would go in there. The hole was only big enough for two of us at a time to fish through, so we we'd chose up sides, two against one, to see who fished first.

Minnie Hall Robbins with Jimmy (left), Wylie and Doug (seated)

When I was little, I used to live there at Shorters Wharf. I wouldn't stay nowheres but with my grandmother Robbins till I started going to school. She thought the world of me.

In the 1940s, while the county built the new bridge, Russell McCollister was courting my Aunt Ruth. He lived over in Cains Ditch and couldn't drive across the river to see Aunt Ruth for some time while that construction went on. So he drove his car to the far side of Shorters Wharf, where he kept a skiff tied up. He untied his skiff, rowed across and got Aunt Ruth and me, and carried us back across to his car. Then we drove to Cambridge to the movies. I always wanted to sit by myself, so he got me popcorn and put me in a seat two or three rows in front of them, where they kept an eye on me. I can't remember Jimmy or Doug saying anything about Aunt Ruth and Uncle Russell just taking me. Being the oldest and the first, I was Aunt Ruth's idol.

***

One old boy around Shorters Wharf loved his beer but didn't like to buy his own. You couldn't say that about a couple of my uncles. Everybody in those days did a lot of walking—not far, but around the little neighborhood there. My uncles walked around drinking Pabst Blue Ribbon, but didn't dare take any to my grandmother's. Even so, she knew when they had beer breath on them.

If they ever had any beer left after their walk, they hid it in a little place under the bridge. They barely had room enough to stoop down there and set the beer up on the sill underneath the bridge. When they went back for their Pabst, they didn't care if it was hot or cold, they drank it. It's a wonder they never fell overboard on a high tide. There wasn't very much room, but they got in and out under that bridge somehow. I believe in later years Jimmy may have used the same spot, but I never started drinking till after I got married and moved away to Elliotts Island.

***

The men on both side of my family were trappers. That goes back at least four generations—probably more. My grandfather Robbins had owned a piece of marsh along the roadside there by the bridge that one of my drinking uncles trapped. He'd come in from fishing his traps and you could tell he'd had some strong drink, but nobody could figure out how he got it. Later we came to understand.

A man named Shorter kept a little store down below and also did some bootlegging. Shorter used to drive down our road past the marsh, stopping at a muskrat house he and my uncle had picked out. To pay for whiskey, my uncle left a couple 'rats he'd trapped for Shorter, and Shorter left the bottle.

I was probably around eight before I knew anything about any drinking going on around there, but I remember both my grandmothers liked to dip snuff. Mamma Robbins dipped the most. She kept a little round tin in the pocket of her apron all the time. Every so often, she took a bit of snuff on her finger and put in her jaw. She may have kept it in her apron to keep us from fooling with it. They both gave it up later on, but I remember them dipping.

***

Mamma Robbins had a big porch like Reese Todd's. On weekends all my uncles and aunts and their friends gathered at her place to sing and play music. There were nine of them Robbinses and they filled that porch up, playing guitars and singing. Uncle Dave was good on the steel guitar. Uncle Joe and my cousin Betty Abbott, Uncle Parks' oldest daughter, won talent contests at the Arcade Theater and State Theater in Cambridge. Betty sang and Uncle Joe played guitar and sang. Those boys were good. Nobody learned them nothing. They picked it up their own selves. Uncle Joe would have gone someplace if he'd tried, but he never did much of nothing. Five or six of them started a group called the Robbins Ramblers that traveled around the county playing here and there. They had guitars, a steel guitar and a fiddle. George

Andrews, who had the Wizard bicycle in school, was the youngest Rambler. George was three years older than me. Uncle Joe taught him to play guitar by counting cadence to him like a drill sergeant.

Probably the first time I ever came to Elliotts Island, I went along when the Robbins Ramblers came over to play in the community building. My father brought us all in his boat. The Blackwater River winds, twisting and turning. twelve miles from Shorters Wharf before coming out into Fishing Bay past Snake Island. Then we sailed down the north shore

Elliott Brothers' crabhouse as it looked in the 1950s.

of the Island to Fishing Point. At that time, the old Elliott Brothers' crabhouse stood at the foot of Elliotts Island Road and had a pier going out. That day a thunderstorm was raising, so Daddy stayed aboard to watch in case a wind might come up and push his boat ashore. You had to watch it there, so he waited with the boat and I went to hear the Ramblers play. Afterwards Daddy carried us all back home across 'the river,' which is what everybody called Fishing Bay.

***

I couldn't do much with music. There wasn't any use in Uncle Joe trying to teach me guitar, but he did teach me how to swim. The Blackwater's deep enough at Shorters Wharf that Uncle Joe used to dive off the top of the draw on the old bridge. Tide runs strong through there, too, and we boys were progging around there all the time. When I was about ten, me and Uncle Joe stood on the bridge one day.

Uncle Joe said, This is a good time to learn how to swim.

With that, he reached over and pushed me overboard. The water came over my head, but I wasn't long coming up thrashing. I heard him hollering down to me.

That's what you gotta do—paddle.

I caught on quick. Not too long after that, when he was only around thirty-three, we learned a disease had come into his back. At that time, just a few ever had whatever disease that was. Too bad Uncle Joe had to be one of them.

He wasn't down in the bed long before he died, but he'd been hurting a lot before that. If he'd ever run into the right person, Uncle Joe would have gone somewhere, but I imagine it's pretty hard to play music and sing hurting like that.

Chapter 6

MR. REESE, A TORNADO AND HURRICANE HAZEL

Reese Todd, who had the boathouse at Shorters Wharf, was a tall, heavy-set man. When we knew him, he was gray-haired and wore glasses. He had a fast way of talking and always had a good word for us boys.

Hey, Dougie, by gawd. Wylie-boy, how y'doin'?

The house where Mr. Reese and Mrs. Cora lived stood just in front of Mamma Robbins', right on the roadside by Shorters Wharf Bridge. The lane next to their house led back to my grandmother's. The second lane from the riverside led back to Sandy Island Cemetery, where lots of my family are buried.

Across the road from his dwelling-house, Mr. Reese had his boathouse—a big building with room enough to work on more than one boat at a time. When he got tired of working on his boats, he went across and sat on his porch to swing for a while.

Me and Jimmy used to bait our lines where the boat ramp is there now. Daddy's little railway was between Mr. Reese's house and my grandmother's. He'd gotten some old railroad tracks somewhere and backed them overboard to haul boats up on, so he could pull a boat up and work on it.

A tornado went through there one time, but it didn't take the boathouse down. I stood in my grandmother's watching it coming. In those days, she had what she called a corn house, a little building to put stuff into. That tornado came down the river, passed by the boathouse, took Mr. Reese's garage, passed his house by, then sent Mamma's corn house skittering right along the ground, the wind picking it up, carrying it along, then setting it down again. I shouldn't have, but I stood in the living room window watching.

***

Skiff pulled up on the site of Winnie Abbott's marine railway, viewed looking towards the rear of Reese Todd's house, with the current bridge over Blackwater River on the right

We boys would go in the boathouse sometimes, when it was raining, or if we wanted to borrow some kind of tool or something. Daddy's brother, Uncle Parks, worked with Mr. Reese some. Daddy worked mostly at the shipyard in town. Uncle Parks did his work at home and did it well.

***

Before having his own boathouse at Shorters Wharf, Mr. Reese had worked at the shipyard in Cambridge. I imagine at one time or another he worked on just about every kind of boat that sailed Chesapeake Bay. When boatbuilding got to be too much, he built boat models people lined up to get.

Mr. Reese was good to deal with as a boatbuilder. Everybody was good to deal with in those days. Prices weren't like now, everybody trying to gouge a dollar out of each other.

Some of the old-timers down there had money though. The most money I ever saw in one place was in 1954, after Hurricane Hazel. My mother was working down to Wingate that October when Hazel came through, flooding south Dorchester. Where we lived stood a little bit high. We seldom saw tide around our house, but most sections down below flooded. Hazel floated two-story houses off their foundations around Bishops Head. People didn't evacuate in those days. One Bramble family's house went sailing, landing them across the road—father and mother, and I think there were two children in the house.

Daddy spent the whole night of Hazel at Farm Creek on his boat. He had her tied up in a little gut off the creek there and he waded down to bail her out and loosen his lines— a ten minute job. By the time he pumped her out and looked around, he couldn't get off. The tide came so quick—what they call the surge—he had to stay aboard letting his lines out and out. Luckily he had a lot of gasoline aboard, because he ran the motor all night to help hold her from breaking the lines. Other boats broke loose and washed in and out the creek and up on the marsh. He stood for hours behind his cabin with a pole, pushing the other boats off so they wouldn't ram into his. He stayed aboard till the tide fell, so he never got off till morning. When it fell, the tide washed out fast, like somebody pulled the plug.

The rest of us stayed home during the storm, but as soon as we could get out we all headed straight for Toddville, where the action was. Everything there got all torn up. Trees blew down in the road. Daddy and everybody were helping others get together whatever they had left.

We were gonna stay two or three nights, till everything got cleared up some, so a friend's parent said, Why don't you boys go up to Will Jones's and stay with him tonight?

Mr. Will was an old man who couldn't hardly hear anything. He lived by himself and they thought he could use some company. When we got there, we found his house made out all right. The water had come in fast and gone out fast.

You had to holler real hard for Mr. Will to hear anything, so we ran to him yelling, *MR. WILL, BOATS IS IN PEOPLE'S BACKYARD!*

Huh?

BOATS IS IN PEOPLE'S BACKYARD!

Huh?

We thought we had some news, but now I know that he'd seen it all before in the August Storm of '33. All together, ten or twelve of us kids stayed there, having a good time. You couldn't make enough racket to disturb Mr. Will.

***

School closed for about a week, till they got things cleaned up a little bit. That time of year, they still picked crabs at George Powley's, where my mother worked. While there was no school, we boys rode the workers' bus to Wingate with Mom. Mr. Powley owned everything around there—the crabhouse, hardware store, grocery, tong boats, dredge boats, the marine railway for his boats and other people's. Mr. Powley treated everybody all right, he just knew how to make money. We'd been going to George Powley's since we were small enough to fit in the crabmeat-can boxes, so Mr. Powley knew us and liked us boys. We always did little chores for him, carrying orders from his grocery store over to the crabhouse, back and forth, things like that.

During Hazel, tide had come over his crabhouse floor, but hadn't done any real damage in there. Over to his dwelling house, though, it got in his safe and soaked his money.

Knowing he didn't have to worry about us, he said, Boys, come along and give me a hand over to the house.

We followed him next door into his kitchen. He opened up his floor safe and there stood stacks of dripping wet bills, all banded up in wide rubber bands. He reached in with both hands, pulling out these stacks, and piled us three boys up with arm-loads of money.

Come on over to the office with me, he said.

We carried them from the house into the office just like we were toting in arms full of cordwood for the stove. We helped spread it out in a little room behind the store. I think after drying it up some, he traded for new money at the bank in Cambridge.

On television every once in a while I see where they've caught some dopers with stacks of bills. It always makes me think of that time, the most money I've seen in one place, before or since.

Chapter 7

When Baker Robbins was County Commissioner, he had his cannery going on Wesley Church Road, where it ran into Andrews from Robbins. He brought that part of the county to life. Baker had big warehouses for his canned goods. Winters he bought fur there and, when the warehouses emptied, he held boxing matches. Dick Shorter, my Island neighbor, used to box there. I was just getting old enough to go to the fights when they cut them off. Ever since, I hate to miss watching a boxing match.

Anyway, Baker was a solid ball of fire and always had some kind of work for us. He had everything going and paid good money. Besides, we couldn't work nowhere else, being too young.

We couldn't hire out for regular work, but when we weren't crabbing, folks knew me and my brothers would take any kind of odd job. A man tilled a field and grew soybeans and corn on Guinea Island, a patch of high land at the head of Fishing Bay. There's no road

Mark Baker Robbins, who operated canneries in Andrews and Vienna with his brothers, rented 10,000 acres of marsh to trappers, and helped found the Outdoor Show.

to Guinea, but he took a Cub Cadet tractor there through Griffiths Neck somehow. He hired me and Jimmy to go up in a boat to pull grass from between the rows. We were maybe twelve and thirteen, working that field in the summer heat.

One day the tractor wouldn't run and Jimmy said, I'll get it goin'. I'll put some of this gasoline on the spark plugs.

Too young to know any better, we cranked her up and the whole darn thing burst into flame. We had nothing to fight the fire with, so we started scooping up sand and throwing it on the tractor like mad. Another day, we sunk his boatload of fertilizer. I guess we weren't cut out to be farmers.

***

Jimmy and Doug were still progging around outside when I got hired at the cannery, working in the warehouse shooting cans. I wasn't big enough yet to lift a case of tomatoes. Shooting cans, I filled up my hands with empty tins, ten at a time, one on each finger, then put them on a conveyor. When they left me, cans went into the tomato department, to the man who took the skinners' full buckets and dumped them into the machine for canning. Then the cans came back towards me to the labeling machine, but I didn't handle full cans.

Once you got used to shooting cans, it was like playing a piano—you got a rhythm going. I could keep that whole cannery going. Being too young to do what I was doing, when we heard an inspector coming, I hid in a box. One summer the boss decided I was big enough, so he put me to loading finished cases onto trucks. At first I thought I was somebody, but before long I wished I was back at my old job. I liked shooting cans.

***

When I grew up, no wild hogs or cows were left, but wild goats still roamed Crab Point, a little piece of high land near the mouth of Honga River. A Gore family had moved from Wesley Church Road to a house up around Cambridge and wanted a couple goats to clean around their yard. Wild goats will eat anything. Daddy had built a workboat for the Gore's son, and they thought of us boys when they wanted some help catching a couple billy goats. We sailed with them from Wingate in the son's workboat and he put us out on Crab Point, which is like a little island with a few trees on it. We started running goats. I was in the lead when this goat came at me—a big old stud with long horns curved back on his head. I reversed myself quick, running right out of my pair of tennis shoes. That goat was closing fast when I shinnied up a tree, grabbing branches and hoisting myself up. I stayed up there till Jimmy and the others came to scare him off.

Finally, we got a hold of two goats and wrestled them aboard the boat, where we tied them up in the cabin. When the engine started up, they went crazy. We heard all this ruckus, then here came a leg through the cabin door. By the time we sailed them back to Wingate, they'd kicked the door off and tore the cabin all up.

I don't know how we ever got those goats on and off that boat, the sides were so high. Mr. Gore was easy-going and didn't say anything when Daddy and Uncle Parks were building her, but Mrs. Gore kept coming outside to the yard.

Build her a little higher, she told them.

They put another board on and Daddy asked her, How's that Miss Daisy? You want to go any farther with her?

Mrs. Gore said, Yeah, go a little farther.

Daddy and Uncle Parks got teased about that boat when they got it done. And it didn't help us any loading goats either.

***

Charlie Willey, who lived up the road from us, liked to brag on his hard head. He was always butting things, so after the goat business, a bunch of us kids went over to see him.

We said, You got a hard head all right, but we bet it ain't as hard as a goat's.

Charlie took his thumb, wiping tobacco juice off the corner of his mouth, and said, Bring a goat over and I'll show you who's got a hard head.

Charlie was all the time breaking doors or basket bottoms or something on his head. On stage at the Outdoor Show, he used to break bricks on his head.

We went and asked Mr. Gore, Can we borrow one of your goats? We want to see if a goat's head is harder than Charlie Willey's.

I don't know, he said. Charlie Willey might kill my goat.

In the end, he let us take a goat, which was still about halfway wild at that time. We got a rope on him, led him to Charlie Willey's place, and lined them up for a showdown.

Charlie had some palsy that caused his head to shake. We lined the goat up about twenty feet from him. Charlie bent forward, his head shaking and goading that goat so bad we could hardly hold him back. That old billy goat was digging his paws in the dirt and throwing his head down. By the time we turned him loose, billy goat was all riled up. It charged and struck the poor man, knocking him out cold. We thought we'd killed Charlie. Somebody ran for water to throw on him and he came around.

I met my match, he admitted.

Chapter 8

TROTLINING

An old boy lived in Robbins named Al Garcia. *GAR-sha* is how we said it. He originally came from somewhere like Arizona, but while he was in the service he met a woman named Maud from Robbins. After he got discharged, they married and settled down home. Being from some desert area out west, he must have thought he'd landed in a hell hole. He didn't know how to do anything around the water, poor fellow. But he learned from scratch and worked at it the rest of his life. Al saw Daddy every day and Daddy and everybody else helped Al pick up how to do.

Al and Maud loved us kids. What we did, we caught minnows for him in little pots we kept in the ditches along the road between Robbins and Shorters Wharf. The ditches were loaded with minnows and we caught a five-gallon bucketful everyday for Al to take out in the river to bait his eelpots. When he and Maud went to the store to get their mail or buy stuff, they always bought something for us boys—candy or cake. If they didn't see us out there along the road that day, they put us something in the mailbox.

After Reese Todd built him a proper workboat, Al let me and Jimmy use this little old sharp-ended skiff he kept tied up at Shorters Wharf. Me and Jimmy always hung around down there around the river. Doug messed with us some, but me and Jimmy were together all the time, doing something. When Al said we could use this 10-foot skiff of his, we started crabbing.

We knew about trotlining crabs, because we'd gone with Daddy since he first came home from the army. That was before he had a car, when he kept his boat tied up at Robbins Landing. We left home around two in the morning to walk back there to the boat, then sail her twelve miles to Fishing Bay. I used to enjoy that walk with Daddy—the stars shining.

Me and Jimmy knew enough already that we could go to work when Al let us have his skiff. We got some chunks of

Double-ender similar to Al Garcia's, this one built on
Elliott Island, displayed with punt gun

wood and rigged up a roller chock to hang over the side. The skiff had two seats. The chock rested on the front seat, one of us standing there with the net, dipping crabs as they came up on the line. We took turns, the other sitting on the back seat paddling. The Blackwater's too deep to pole around Shorters Wharf.

We got bait—tripe—that we kept on the bank by the bridge salted down in a pickle barrel, big hairy slabs of cow belly. You could leave anything anywhere and nobody would bother it. The tripe we used was brown and stunk terrible, but made the best kind of crab bait. Every day we'd bait up our lines, one of us laying a slab over the rim of the barrel slicing off chunks while the other baited the line. Nowadays tripe's in the supermarket, cleaned up in the meat counter, and you can't afford to use it for bait.

We had a second barrel to put our catch into—55-gallon barrels, they were. We had old lead window weights to anchor the ends of the line when we put it overboard. Anytime we found a plastic jug, we latched on to that for a buoy, or else we used a piece of wood.

We kept at it, crabbing every day it wasn't blowing, till we were buying tripe by the 200-pound barrel and making sixty to seventy-five dollars a week. The skiff couldn't hold that many crabs, so we'd go ashore and put some on the bank while we went back out for more. We had them in baskets or barrels, whatever we could get. A barrel loaded with crabs was heavy, maybe 150 pounds. We neither one ever grew to be real big, but we were wiry little guys at that time. We rolled them or wrestled them onto the bank someways. One week we made over a hundred dollars. Me and Jimmy were the talk of the town.

Nights, you could go in any store down below and that's all you'd hear, Them Abbott boys, did you hear what they caught today?

In those days, nobody else fooled much with crabbing the Blackwater around Shorters Wharf, but certain times of the year lots of crabs go up that river. They go out when it's rainy and the water gets too fresh. Other times, when the men weren't catching nothing 'out front,' which meant Fishing Bay, we boys were up the river catching crabs.

***

We sold our catch and bought our bait about ten miles from Shorters Wharf, from Bernard Murphy at Farm Creek, where Daddy had his boat tied up and sold his crabs. Daddy had his 1946 Ford pickup then and helped us get our catch and bait back and forth. We got a block of ice from the crabhouse and we had a little cooler we took in the skiff. We carried Royal Crowns or Pepsi, and Mom packed our dinner in a lard can, ham or scrapple sandwiches, anything she had.

The skiff was good and tight, but not four foot across at the widest. She tapered down, sharp-pointed on both ends, so it didn't take much to turn her over. One day early on, we got arguing and fighting. We'd laid our lines out, buoys on each end, and picked the line up onto the roller. I was the oldest, the captain, but I let Jimmy take the first turn dipping crabs while I paddled.

After Jimmy missed the first couple crabs, I started fussing—something smart like, I'll dip 'em myself if you can't do no better than that.

Oh yeah? says Jimmy—always scrappy.

Yeah, you go on missin' 'em and you can paddle, I said.

I'd like to see you make me.

We started tussling and turned the whole mess over upside down, us in the river snatching for paddles and chock and baskets. Luckily, we had our lines laid out already or we could have been in a tangle. We hadn't caught the first crab yet, either, so didn't lose nothing. Only the bow of the crab net started sinking, and that had a long handle we could grab onto. We kicked and pushed, shoving the skiff over to a mud-flat so we could flip her back up to bail her out.

We didn't have many episodes like that, though a lot of temptations comes along over the years for two brothers in that kind of work. You've got to have good nerves, looking at that water all day long. Some brothers don't get along together like me and Jimmy did. Maybe that day taught us something that stuck with us.

***

The Blackwater River snakes every-which-way. They could see us from land at Shorters Wharf if we stayed in The Broads, the reach above the bridge, or in Backgarden Creek Reach, the one below. In time we worked our way farther and farther up and down the river. We ran two short lines of two hundred yards each, about as long as those reaches are, putting one in one reach and one in the next. When the crabs fell off there, we jumped on down a couple reaches, till we were laying our lines all the way below Robbins Landing. Coming back with our crabs, we'd try to catch a fair tide, both of us pulling, using all the paddle-power we could muster.

To let my kids out in a skiff like that would have worried me right to death, but the old man let us go. The bank was never too far away, always somewhere we could swim to.

We watched a man drown there one day, though, right at Shorters Wharf. We were on the bank baiting up, Doug with us helping. We heard this truck coming, gears shifting. We looked over at this dump truck starting up the far side of the bridge, then we heard loud, loud crackling and snapping. He carried a load of sand and was too heavy. His back wheels busted through the decking, then the truck slid right on back, through the bridge and into the river. It's deep there, maybe twenty feet.

I said, Oh my God, get Mr. Reese.

Reese Todd generally worked by himself, but that day he had another man inside the boathouse helping—Uncle Parks, I believe.

We ran in there yelling, Mr. Reese! Mr. Reese! There's a truck gone through the bridge!

They ran out looking and Mr. Reese said, By gosh, Wylie-boy, it is! We gotta take the skiff and try to get the man out of 'er.

They took our skiff and paddled out. They aimed to get the man out the driver's side window, but they couldn't barely reach him or get him loose. We stood there watching, holding our breath. It's hard when there's nothing you can do, just stand on the bank and look. Finally, they had to give it up and come back and call on Mr. Reese's phone for help. Crews came from every direction then. We saw the truck pulled out of the river, the driver still in there. It's bad to see something like that happen. I guess that's one reason I don't think much of that Transquaking River bridge. I don't go over there unless I have to.

Chapter 9

After sixth grade I rode the county school bus to Crapo. The county was building South Dorchester High School in Golden Hill at the time, but it wasn't done. Everybody from down below too old for grade school went to Crapo. I went there for seventh grade, then after that to South Dorchester High School, where Mr. Goldie Tyler was principal.

The first assignment I got from the shop teacher, Mr. Hubbard, was to make Mr. Tyler a paddle. Mr. Hubbard told me just how to make it. I had to drill holes every inch, so Mr. Tyler could swing it faster. The paddle wasn't especially for me, just one to keep in the principal's office.

While I worked on it, I said to the next guy, I bet I'm the first one to get this sumbitch.

Mr. Tyler taught class as well as being our principal. Sure enough, we got to cutting up in his class one day.

Wylie, he said, go to my office. I'll be down in a few minutes.

I knew just what was coming, but he gave me a few minutes to think about it. While I waited, I got smart and stuck a book down the seat of my britches.

When Mr. Tyler came in, he said, Bend over that desk.

I bent over ready for him and he said, Oh no. None of that. Get that book out of there.

So that's what I did, and he tore my tail up. I guess he paddled me two or three times over the years, but I liked him anyway. He was a good teacher. I cut up in class, showing off too much. I'd discovered girls.

***

– 45 –

A girl named Edna may have been my first little crush, but she was from the crabhouse, not from school. Edna was

Wylie Abbott

four or five years older than me, a pretty, black-haired girl. I remember a day came when I was about twelve. I didn't go out messing around with Jimmy and Doug. I stayed in the crabhouse all day cracking claws 'cause I had the stool alongside of Edna and she was nice to me. I didn't want to get up and have somebody take my seat. I cracked fifteen pounds of claw meat that day. We got 16-cents a pound cracking claws at that time, the same as crab pickers got.

***

A preacher ran a little community center for the kids in Crapo we liked to go to if we could get a ride. We used to play ping-pong, stuff like that. When I was a little older, I figured out that most girls liked to dance, so I wasn't one of the boys hanging back. I could dance.

***

Besides girling, driving was the other thing on my mind. At about thirteen, me and my cousin, Junior North, toted muskrats out of the marsh for his father and Daddy, who had 1,200 acres of marsh rented back behind Bounds Church. As they trapped, Daddy and Herbert North Sr. left bundles of 'rats in there for me and Junior to pick up. After school we went and collected them, took them home, and skinned them. Daddy let me use his old 1946 Ford pickup. This one day Mamma Robbins needed a lift. I had her on the front seat with me and Junior North and Jimmy in the back of the pickup.

I held the turn near our house too wide and ran us in the ditch. I was scared to death I'd throw Junior or Jimmy out, but when I popped back up on the road, they were still in there and laughing about it all.

A guy who lived down that way was coming from the other direction at nearly the same time. He came a fraction later, but my grandmother swore he ran us off the road.

Jimmy Abbott

I said, Mamma, I ran in the ditch. I ran Daddy's truck right in there myself.

She said, I saw that Otis Todd. He ran you off the road.

She was still taking my side while I carried her on home. The truck just had a little mud on it and I used the water hose on that and Daddy didn't say nothing. In fact, I don't remember that he ever paddled me or my brothers either one. When we weren't in school, we were too busy working to get in much trouble.

***

Muskrats were thick then where Daddy and Uncle Herbert worked together. Uncle Herbert had married Daddy's sister Oceola. Besides the 1,200 acres behind the church he and Daddy rented, Daddy had Jobes Point, another 600 acres going towards Cambridge. They had a thousand traps and took 180 to 200 'rats a day. That's how I got to be so fast, from skinning all those muskrats. The last year we all did that together, they caught 3,700 muskrats by the fifth of February. Then the bottom fell out of the market and they had to quit.

I set a few traps on my own—just enough to last me from after school till dark. Then I went to the garage and skinned.

Those Norths were strong men. In those days, they strung muskrats up fifty in a bunch. One day coming out of the marsh. Uncle Herbert had fifty and Daddy took fifty. That's well over a hundred pounds a bundle. Daddy was strong for his size, but he wasn't very big—about the size I am now. Uncle Herbert was over six foot tall and could stand a lot of work. My old man thought he was jacked down with fifty 'rats.

When they got to hard ground, Herbert said, Oh hell, give me that bundle.

He had his fifty on one side and threw Daddy's fifty on the other and brought a hundred of them out of there saying, Come on boy, this is how you do it.

Thirty or thirty-five were more than I ever wanted in my time. You go through the marsh with thirty on your back, you know you've done something.

Herbert's Uncle Jim over to Cains Ditch was another strong man. If a car ran into the ditch, he'd lift it right out. To drive pilings for the new Shorters Wharf bridge, a barge tied up by the boathouse carrying a crane with a big ball to pound them down. Jim North lifted that ball, said to weight over nine hundred pounds. Folks said Jim North lifted a barrel of molasses in the store one night and both his feet went through the floor.

***

All those people around there could cook muskrat, potted down in gravy, meat falling off the bone. Talk about right, my mother could cook a muskrat. I was wolfing it down once when I was small and choked on a bone lodged in my throat. They rushed me all the way to Cambridge and just as we got to the hospital, I popped it out.

Mamma Abbott could cook all those wild things. When she was around sixty, Daddy brought her out to live by the roadside. He and his brothers built her a little house right alongside ours. Nellie Willey was still alive then. She'd been company for their mother for years, so they built a room onto Mamma's little house for Nellie to sleep in, but I don't think Nellie lived a month after they brought her out from Robbins Landing.

When some of the boys got old enough to drive around, I took off with them. If I got home late, I'd see Mamma Abbott's light still on next door. After I got upstairs to bed and turned my light off, I'd see hers go off. Next day I'd be laying in bed and hear her come in downstairs.

Dorothy, she'd say, that boy's gonna get in trouble. He never got in this morning till two o'clock.

He'll be all right, Mom said.

My grandmother Abbott lived to be seventy and her hair never turned grey, except for a couple little sprigs. The only way I remember her is with a long dark ponytail.

***

Before everybody could afford a car, Albert Kirwin had two or three buses going Saturday nights from all over down below into Cambridge. My mother could drive a car when she wanted to go to town, but neither grandmother drove. When I got to high school and turned sixteen, Mamma Robbins got me a 1949 Mercury—straight shift, overdrive, good on gas. She gave $250 for that car and I paid her back when I could. I rode both my grandmothers around. Being a young boy with a car to drive, I loved to do that.

That car of mine ran like a top and got good gas mileage, too, but I didn't much like its looks. A boy from Cambridge had a 1951 Mercury convertible and I went and traded the sedan for that convertible.

In those days not many girls had cars. If you saw a girl driving, you looked at her till she got out of sight. Generally, girls always needed rides and I loaded that convertible up with them, two loads a day. The convertible was a lemon, though. Everything in the world tore up on it. I didn't keep it over a month.

***

Those were good old days and we didn't appreciate them while they were going on. A gallon of gas was 18-cents. All I wanted to do was work, so I didn't have to worry about gas money. We made big money on the water in those days. That's what caused me to quit school like a fool. I've had a lot of opportunities in my days I could have taken if I'd gone back to school, but instead I went logging.

***

I did a good bit of logging with Russell McCollister, my uncle who used to take me to the movies while courting Aunt Ruth. Wintertime, when Uncle Russell wasn't farming, he logged. Usually, it was just him and me. If he got jammed up with a big order, he might get another man—usually Johnny Willey or Francis Pinder, good workers.

Logging is where I hurt my back. One day I sawed a big old tree down, that chain saw rattling my teeth. I landed her and went to sit down on the stump and rest up. My back got a catch right across it and ain't been right since. I sat awhile, then went to get up, and I couldn't move. That chainsaw was a little bit too big a one for me at sixteen.

Another day, I don't know where my uncle was that he didn't see what I was doing. I cut down a tree about twenty feet tall and it lit into another tree without coming down all the way. I crawled up the trunk and was gonna jump off when my weight brought it down, but it fell too fast. I couldn't get away when the thing cut loose. Lucky it jumped away instead of on top of me, but right between my legs chafed red as fire from sliding down. Logging is a hard and dangerous job.

***

Like all Mom's sisters, Aunt Ruth was real nice, and she'd feed me everyday. Uncle Russell gave me $25 a week and filled my tank up with gas, good money in those days. A tankful lasted me the whole week, plus a little bit more. Monday was Uncle Russell's day to relax. I'd ride him around all day on Monday anywhere he wanted to go—usually where he could get something cold to drink. Bucktown was the biggest place. I've seen him spend the whole day right there.

The woods we worked stood right alongside the yard, close to Aunt Ruth's flowers. I came out one day on a tractor, dragging a loaded logging cart. I wasn't paying attention and drug right through her flower bed. She loved those flowers. She got right down into them and cried when she saw what I'd done. Oh man, I never got close to that yard no more.

Chapter 10

THE DOVETAIL

Most of Daddy's brothers were house carpenters in Cambridge, but Daddy and Uncle Parks built boats. If they wanted a boat, they built a boat. Sometimes Daddy helped Reese Todd, but mostly built at boatyards in Cambridge or Oxford. He built boats at our house, too, right there in our yard, if anybody came along wanting one. He had carts made up to haul them to the river, any size boat up to around forty feet. He put them overboard by the Shorters Wharf Bridge.

Me and Jimmy were thirteen and fourteen when they built us a man-sized boat. An old wreck lay up on the bank at Shorters Wharf—a big boat about 40-foot long. Daddy and Uncle Parks cut her into three parts and made me and Jimmy a boat out of it. They took out the middle section that was rotten and joined the bow and stern pieces into a 28-foot boat—big in those days for anybody. Before they went to work on her, she was a regular square-sterned power boat, but they made her into a dovetail. I guess they just wanted to see what they could do. She was a sharp-looking thing when they got her done. Daddy got us an inboard 6-cylinder Chevrolet motor and set her up with everything we needed.

That old boat probably had thirty years on her when she got put up on the bank to rot away. Daddy and Uncle Parks didn't pay nothing for it; the person gave it to them. She'd have never floated again if they hadn't done what they did. A wooden boat rots quick if you don't take care of it. They took twelve feet out of her, nailed a bottom on her and turned her over right where she'd died, about fifty yards upriver from the bridge. Those old people could do anything.

When me and Jimmy got that dovetail, we thought, This is no boat we got now. We got us a ship.

Tongers on Fishing Bay aboard dovetail similar to that built by Winnie and Parks Abbott. Pictured here around 1960 are Wylie's Island neighbors Will Horsman, store owner Alonzo "Gittle" Gray, and the dovetail's captain Randall Ewell

The adventures on the dovetail marked our real starting out on the water. We were finally ready for our first sail out beyond Blackwater River—first down reaches we knew like Backgarden Creek, Robbins Landing, Snare Pole Gut, Ther'fer [Thoroughfare], then farther than we'd ever been before. Altogether, we needed to sail twelve miles to Fishing Bay, then around to Farm Creek, where Daddy harbored.

That first May morning, we put our gear aboard and Daddy checked us out.

Where's your gasoline?

We got our can up there, we said, pointing to a gallon can sitting by the road.

You boys would start across Chesapeake Bay with a gallon of gasoline, he said, shaking his head.

He'd get on us, but we needed it. His own boat was still on his railway. He got us more gasoline off of it. He explained to us how to go. We just had to follow the river, bearing left at Stingers Bend to stay out of Raccoon Creek, then we couldn't go wrong. Next morning, we'd be crabbing 'out front' in Fishing Bay, like Daddy and the other men.

We took off, running down river, past Reese Todd's and Mamma Robbins'. We went past Uncle Wes' pound nets and Robbins Landing, where Mamma Abbott's house had burned down some years earlier. The river doubled back on itself time and again. We bore away from Raccoon Creek, which led back up to Uncle Parks' house on Robbins Road. When we came out the mouth of the river by Snake Island into Fishing Bay, we ran our lines out to try the crabs. We used shorter lines than they do now and we could keep them on crabs better. We caught three or four baskets. By then, it was around three o'clock, so we pulled our lines up and headed for Farm Creek. Right off Blackwater Point, we ran across some deer swimming across Fishing Bay—one of them a big buck.

Jimmy said, Let's get one of them.

I said, All right, we'll get him. Let me get you up close and you take something to hit him with.

Man, we got up there and Jimmy leaned over the side and grabbed that big buck's rack and flipped him over the washboard into the boat. Jimmy had him on the deck holding his head down and that buck a-kicking. I was trying to catch his legs, but he kicked and broke the engine box loose. It's a wonder he didn't cut us up or kill us both, but Jimmy still hung on with both hands.

I said, Jimmy, let's get rid of this thing. If we don't turn him loose quick, he's gonna tear the boat up.

Somehow or other, we bailed him back overboard without getting our brains kicked out of us. We went on into Farm Creek and tied up. Everything came through all right except the engine box. The men around there couldn't believe what we'd done when we told them.

Daddy came down to pick us up, saw the boat, and said, You boys could tear up hell.

We put the engine box back together and next morning we were down to Farm Creek early, rearing to go. First crabs of the year, I don't remember how many we caught, but we did good.

We went on crabbing the dovetail together like that till we were grown and Jimmy went in the Army. By that time, I'd already married and, when he left, the dovetail shifted over to me to crab alone.

***

I was sailing out from Farm Creek one morning by myself, down Goose Creek shore. when I smelled gas. I looked under that engine box and she was a solid blaze of fire. I had a regular car's gas tank into her leaking. It's a wonder she didn't blow up. The only thing saved me, she was an open boat and didn't create fumes. Gasoline won't make an explosion; the fumes do. All I did, I poured water on the exhaust pipe up close to where the fire burned. I didn't want to tear up nothing. I turned around and went back in the creek. A hole had come into my gas tank. The old car tanks weren't worth the devil. They'd get a pinhole into them and leak into the bilge, then you got a fire.

***

The last I knew of the dovetail, Doug had her and used her two or three years to play around into, then he sold her to somebody from Taylors Island. From there she went up the Bay somewhere. Later in life, Jimmy got himself another dovetail to work off of.

Chapter 11

TONGING OYSTERS

I don't remember what age I started oystering with Daddy, but I know I couldn't reach the cull board he set across his boat for sorting small oysters out of the catch. Daddy turned a wooden pop case over and I stood on that, working leaning against the board. I wasn't over seven or eight, going with him whenever I wasn't in school. During the week, he took somebody else. Weekends or holidays, I'd take their place. Men traded around so everybody always had somebody onboard with them when they went out oystering. A man doesn't need to be out by himself in the wintertime, standing on a workboat's washboard tonging up oysters.

When I first went along to cull for him, Daddy wasn't long home from the war, because we didn't have a car yet. We walked to Robbins Landing, where he kept his boat tied up across the marsh from his mother's house. We sailed from there down the Blackwater and out to the oyster rocks in Fishing Bay. Oysters were supposed to be three inches, but the state had no limit on a man's catch then that I know of. A winter day has only so much daylight, though. After oystering, we landed our catch at Farm Creek, gassed up, then had to come all the way back upriver and straighten up the boat. His mother would have something fixed for us to eat, a nice meal, with homemade bread—biscuits or yeast rolls. She loved doing that, just loved it. Then we walked home from Robbins Landing to Robbins under the stars. When Jimmy got a little bigger, he went with us. On the boat, we were all business.

At around fourteen, I started tonging, doing what I had watched Daddy do. I copied his actions, up on the washboard working the shafts and pulling them up hand-under-hand. You don't need long arms when oysters are nice and thick—shafts don't need to open real wide to fill up the rakes.

Tong shafts are pinned together anywhere from midway to one-third way down towards the heads, depending on how long they are. There's no difference in how they work except for pulling them back up after you got your lick of oysters in the rakes. Around Fishing Bay we used mostly 16s or 20s, but we tonged with shafts as long as 26-feet in deeper spots. A 26 is a lot of wood to pull up.

***

One day in our teens, we were out in Fishing Bay working Ther'fer Rock, Jimmy tonging off one side, me off the other, while Dad culled. We'd just had a freeze, but this morning came bright sunny for January. The river was still icy cold, but thawed. I got sweating and jumped down in the boat and took my coat off. I tossed it in the cabin, and hopped back up on the washboard. I was working my rakes again when I heard an airplane flying towards us. Walking backwards to dump my lick on the cull board, I watched it get bigger and bigger as it neared us—a kind of plane I hadn't seen before.

That's a funny-looking airplaaa..., I started saying, and Balooop, I walked right off the stern of the boat.

Daddy had been looking down culling, but he saw me go over out of the corner of his eye, or he heard me splash, 'cause he called out to Jimmy, Grab Wylie!

That cold water shocked me and the tide was running strong. I kicked my boots off, grabbed my tongs, and paddled up to the stern of the boat where the rudder blade sticks out.

Jimmy was still up on the washboard and I heard him say, Wait till I make this lick and set my tongs down.

Hell with tongin', I hollered. This water's cold!

Before Jimmy set his tongs down, I got my knee up on the rudder blade and raised myself up and came over the stern. I still had hold of my tongs and pulled them in after me. When they had me back aboard, Dad just shook his head. For my part, I welcomed those warm, dry clothes I'd peeled off earlier.

Daddy would often stick his jaw out a little and shake his head saying, I don't know where he gets it from.

People said, though, that there was no difference between us.

***

I tonged with Joe Gray, my future father-in-law, as a teenager, before I got married. He owned oyster beds right behind his father's place. His father, 'King David' Gray, lived close to the marsh just above Elliotts Island. When oystering season closed in the spring on public rock, we tonged Joe's private beds in Fishing Bay behind King David's.

Joe had an old dugout canoe, the *River Queen,* he kept just for tonging. Between times, he ran it into the Upper Creek and let it sink by the edge of the marsh near the Island bridge. When oystering was coming back in, he'd go bail her out and she'd pop back up again. Every year or so he'd go up to a junkyard in Cordova and get a Ford engine for her.

We had walking boards on her. A canoe didn't have washboards you could stand on like a plank-built workboat has. Aboard the *River Queen*, we stood on walking boards and reached across the side. It helped to be able to brace your knees swinging the tongs in over the cull board to dump your lick, but working from washboards is a little easier.

Working on Joe's oyster beds, we could get fifty or sixty bushels in two hours. We sold to Miles Rhodes, who sailed the buy-boat *Shamrock* from Chincoteague, Virginia up to Fishing Bay. He loaded his oysters in Fishing Bay and plugged right on back to his home port, about a three hour sail. Miles Rhodes gave us a little more money than some other buyers, plus Joe got a big drink off of him.

Miles would say, Wylie, will you have one?

Joe Gray tonging from his dugout canoe
River Queen *around 1960*

I didn't drink in those days. Plus I was bucking for son-in-law and wouldn't have said yes in front of Joe anyway.

Buy-boats bought a lot of our catch. When I started working on the water, more market boats than trucks carried the catch. At one time, there might have been fifteen buy-boats a season coming in from Tangier Sound to Fishing Bay or sailing out from the Island. We went to them with our catch. Sometimes if there were many boats unloading, they started sailing with us still hooked on to them. Then they started trucking more and more every year till the market boat was no more.

***

Tonging oysters for hours like that takes something out of a man, I don't care how strong he is. In fact, strength doesn't have all that much to do with it. Tonging is an art, and if you don't have the knack for it, strength doesn't help. Darius

Horsman came from up to Henrys Crossroads, a big, strong guy, but tonging was too much for him.

Darius got about three licks up on the board one day and said, Carry me ashore. I'll not do this.

He went down to Chincoteague and got a trawler.

After you pull and haul gripping that tong shaft all day, your muscles swell up in your hands and arms. I thought something ailed me when I first had this numbness. I went to the doctor about it.

He said, Nothing's wrong with you. It's just that your muscle's not relaxed.

Evenings, you'd have to sit in your chair or sleep against the head of the bed with your hands hanging down, trying to loosen them up and get blood flowing and get feeling back.

People who aren't born into it can learn. I've seen it done, but most don't want to work that hard.

***

Dad was known for working long shafts. I picked up his 26s when he put them down. I worked them mostly on slack water, when they're not so hard to handle. When that tide's running, you know you're pulling on something with 26s. You have to hold them just right, so they balance when you pull them up.

When oysters were scarce, I used those 26s working Bungys, a hole out here at the mouth of the creek—just outside the Island harbor. Even with 26s, to work Bungys I had to stand down on the bottom of the boat and reach over with my hands in the water—damn cold, but you had to take it. Instead of tonging all day to get five bushels, I could go in that deep water and catch ten or fifteen bushels in an hour. If Jimmy's father-in-law, Rodney Robinson, wasn't there, I had it all to myself. There were plenty of big old oysters at Bungys. You could open and shut the rakes a couple times and you had your lick.

Maybe I had an edge on the guys who didn't trap. I worked with my hands in cold water everyday of trapping season. A lot of trappers get arthritis bad, but I've been lucky that way.

***

When we quit at the end of the oyster season in the spring of 1962, we were still nearly catching our limit, plus there was a load of little oysters. Everybody counted on a big season when oystering opened back up that fall, but that water's got to be just right. I was the first one to find a load of dead oysters off Elliotts Island that year.

I always went out ahead of time checking them. Sometime in August or early in September, 1962, I went out in front of the harbor and tried those little hills. I tried Bungys and Old House and Ther'fer. All the oysters on those rocks had died. I tried over to the mouth of Farm Creek, where we had big hills, and went around different places upriver and found it the same everywhere.

I came back in and told the Island boys, Oysters are gonna be scarce this year. It's gonna be rough goin'.

They didn't believe me They said, All them pretty oysters can't all be dead.

An oyster's got to have the water just right. They filter so much all the time and can't get away when something gets in there that's not right. They're stuck on that rock filtering that poisoned water.

Chapter 12

ELLIOTTS ISLAND

When I was fifteen, not old enough to have a license yet, my cousin Theodore came by one day and said, Me and Mom are goin' to a party over to Elliotts Island. You wanna ride over with us?

I said, Yeah, I'll ride with you.

He said, They're having a party for my cousin Louella's fourteenth birthday.

Theodore's mother, Inez, was a North before she married my father's cousin Arthur. Inez's sister, Helen North Gray, had married an Islander and they were having a big beach party for their daughter's birthday. That's when me and Louella met and started seeing each other. Theodore dated a friend of hers on the Island, Georgene Martinek. After that party, we started driving around there from Robbins together.

Daddy got a brand-new '55 Buick while this was going on, and he let me drive that new car. It took an hour to get from Robbins around to Elliotts Island, and a lot of those roads that circled around Fishing Bay weren't paved. A stretch at Henrys Crossroads was always torn up—had a dip in the road where water lay, and sand and mud. I remember high tides with Theodore riding on the Buick's hood, pushing off trees floating across the road. He'd use his feet to keep them from hitting and messing up the car. We'd hit other stuff, or pick it up along the way.

Daddy said, You never know what them boys are gonna have in the car trunk.

Sometimes he'd open his trunk and we had deer or 'coons or most anything. This went on for a couple years, till Louella finished school. I was running the road all night long. My courting wasn't very easy.

One night me and Theodore were driving home from Elliotts Island and saw a ghost light. We were near about to Shorters Wharf about three o'clock in the morning.

I said, That looks like a ghost light over there, coming across the marsh.

He saw it too for a few minutes, then it went away. It was going right straight for Sandy Island graveyard, but went out before it got there. I never did see any more. I think that must've been marsh gas.

***

As a little kid lying in bed upstairs in my grandmother Robbins' house at Shorters Wharf, I used to watch the lights of cars going on Elliotts Island. I never imagined I'd ever live there, but I always did like the Island, from the first time I came here. You had a lot of old people to fool with on here then.

At the last going off before me and Louella got married, I stayed on the Island more than at home. Robert Hurley lived on the Island and let me use his boat crabbing, or I oystered with Louella's father, Joe Gray.

Over to Farm Creek, the watermen were already out in the river when the sun came up. A lot of the old people over on the Island wouldn't come out till nine o'clock. The watermen from the other side called the Islanders The Sons of Rest. I thought to myself, those Islanders are on to something.

***

The first year or so we were married, Louella moved to Robbins. Till we got our house on the Island built, we lived in the little house Daddy had built for his mother. Daddy's youngest brother, my Uncle Josh, was building our Island house. Uncle Josh was the nicest man you'd ever meet. He didn't just slap something together. She's a well-built house and cost me $8,100 to build on land next to Joe Gray's house. Four or five Abbotts worked on building our house, uncles and cousins, and they weren't long putting it up. Elihu and Ted's father, Arthur Abbott, worked on it. Arthur Abbott was slow, but he did good work. He had hands so big, I've seen his gloves bust right out when he made a fist. Uncle Josh was an able man. When he got to be eighty years old, he still climbed rooftops.

***

While the house was going up, Jimmy left and went in the army. Our brother Doug never did care as much about progging, but me and Jimmy had always been together all our lives up till then. People who didn't know us well took us for twins. When he left, I was digging a darn trench by hand from the road to the new house for the waterline. I missed Jimmy so much, I'd dig awhile and cry awhile. Every time I'd take a shovelful of dirt, I'd sit down and cry. The only time me and Jimmy ever were apart was when he went in the army.

When Uncle Josh finished and the house was all hooked up, we moved from Robbins to the Island. After that, one of my cousins towed Mamma Abbott's house with a tractor ten miles down the road on skids, from Robbins to Toddville.

***

I kept on working the dovetail while our house was being built. To save money on buying bait, I cleaned a pound netter's boat out for him in trade for any hogchokers he caught. Hogchokers are like little flounder. I cut them in half and rolled them up to bait my trotline. I drove a '51 Chevy and had a little trailer I pulled with a couple barrels on it for the fish. One day I filled the barrels and still had a pile of hogchokers. I couldn't stand to waste them, so I pulled the rear seat out and shoveled the back of the car full of fish.

Doug was with me that day. Driving home with all those fish, we came up on a fire. Police were directing traffic and I didn't have a good tag for my trailer.

While we waited to be waved on, I told Doug, Get out and sit on the trailer and hang your foot over the license.

The cop waved us on by. If he'd stuck his head inside the Chevy that summer day, he wouldn't have been surprised Doug didn't want to ride with those fish.

We'd try most anything to save on bait. One year Daddy salted down his muskrat tails, but he didn't have much luck with them.

***

For a couple years, me and Louella didn't have any children. I remember a cousin of ours buying oysters over to Farm Creek at that time. Me and Daddy were putting out oysters there one day.

My cousin asked me, Wylie, you got any kids yet?

Daddy spoke up, No. I think he's gonna die with his seed in him.

Once they started, though, they kept coming. Me and Louella had three, Wylie Jr., Wendy and Robert. Cory came along later by my second wife, Teresa.

***

When I moved onto Elliotts Island, Hob Horseman had an old double-ended skiff there, like the one Al Garcia had given me and Jimmy to get us started. That's the last one I saw used every day. Hob kept his big workboat tied off Red Hill on the north shore of the Island. He used his double-ender to push out to it. Nobody's tied up on that side of the Island in forty-some years and Hob wasn't the last one, so it's longer than that since I saw one of those double-enders used every day, like me and Jimmy used ours.

The last one to tie up off Red Hill was Gilbert Gray. Most of us put our boats inside the Lower Creek. There wasn't any water to speak of in there at McCready Creek at the start, but we kept running our boats in and the wheels from our props made a deeper channel. The old-timers had Palmers or air-cooled engines on their dugout canoes that they tied up in there. Palmers had that old big wheel you turned with your hand to start it. No more than two pulls and she'd go. Blooom, blooom, then she let out a big blow when she caught. Those air-cooled, though, they were hard. The old air-cooled had a reel on it like a grass cutter and you pulled the rope to start it. Mornings all up and down there to the creek you'd hear different ones when they pulled the cord trying to start their air-cooled.

When it didn't catch, it went, Sshhh.

Then you'd hear, Go to Hell.

Someone tried again and, Sshhh.

If that thing backfired when he pulled her, she'd near about pull his fingers off; then you'd hear, Oh, Shit!

We used the Lower Creek free for

Wylie trotlining in Fishing Bay off Elliotts Island

nothing till the county took it over in the '70s and built a harbor of sorts. They started charging slip rental, but aside from a couple slips, they're still not worth much of anything.

They could've designed it a lot better if they'd talked to the old guys who used it day in and day out.

***

There were a lot more people on the Island at that time. We had enough young people to field a softball team called the Elliott Seahawks. The Seahawks came within a game of winning the league championship in 1964. Nobody thought we could play ball like that and they didn't like it much when we beat them. The Seahawks didn't do no practicing. We just piled in two or three cars on Sunday and went. Playing places over river like Toddville, we could have gone in a boat, but some of us wanted to stop on the way home at the little general store run by that Shorter, the bootlegger who used to leave bottles for my uncle. He didn't stock much in the food line, but he could give you most anything else you wanted.

Our home games we played here at the schoolhouse, where the firehouse is now. Those other teams hated to come here and play.

They'd say, We're goin' down and play in that watermelon patch.

You never knew which way the ball would bounce. If you hit a ball good, it went into the woods and there was the mosquitoes.

The last day of the season, we had to go to Cambridge and play a night doubleheader against Wire Cloth. We never played under lights before and fielders lost fly balls in the lights. Hitters couldn't meet the ball. We lost both ends of the doubleheader and the league title.

Chapter 13

MY NEW WORKBOAT

While me and Louella lived in the house that had been my grandmother Abbott's, waiting for our Island house to be finished, I didn't have any idea of needing a new boat. The plan had been for me to keep the dovetail and Daddy to build a boat for Jimmy, so we'd each have our own. Then Jimmy up and went in the army. Daddy already had the lumber in his boathouse, so he decided to build her for me instead—all cedar and white oak she was.

I blew her up in 1960, the same year he built her. It happened around the end of August, on a Sunday night. Most watermen didn't go out on a Sunday in those days, but I had to hustle every day I could. I crabbed all night, Sunday into Monday, catching a solid ton by daybreak, when my engine cut out. About that time, Henry Jones came out to start crabbing near where I stalled, and he gave me a jump.

I had an extra five-gallon can of gasoline I always carried aboard on the floor of the cabin, behind the bottled gas for my little cookstove. Crabs were everywhere and I picked up that gasoline can and propped it on top of the bottled gas to get it out of the way. After Henry jump-started me, I revved my engine, made a circle, picked up my line, and dropped it in the chock. I ran about half-way down the line and, Whoomp. . .

All I knew, I was standing there in my short rubber boots steering her and dipping crabs, then I heard that noise. Next thing I knew, I'd blown right out of my boots. I came to myself overboard, and something had told me to start swimming. As I was paddling back to the boat, Darius Horsman from Henrys Crossroads was nearby. He told me later I blew fifteen feet in the air. I don't remember going out of her, but I'm glad I came down in the water instead of landing on my boat somewhere The explosion stalled the motor out. I saw her burning, dead in the water, a rough looking sight to see, coming to yourself overboard. The one thing on my mind was to get that fire out and save my boat. We'd just built her and I had my heart in her.

I figured out later that the gasoline can tipped off when I made that turn, the cap cracked, and gas leaked under the floorboards into the bilges. We didn't have alternators then and the generators we had could raise a big spark.

I had a fire extinguisher on the back of the engine box and another one in the cabin. I hauled myself up till I could see over the side. Solid flame is all I saw. I wasn't scared for a minute. It hadn't got me up tight, but I was afraid she'd blow again. She still had one washboard I could walk onto and I hauled myself up on that. All the cabin was gone and part of my crabs—the crabs in baskets. Twelve or fifteen barrels of crabs were still aboard. I jumped down onto the deck and grabbed the extinguisher off the engine box and knocked down the fire around the box above deck. Then I ran forward after the second extinguisher. The cabin stood open to the sky—windows and roof gone, except for the broken glass I was running on. I grabbed the fire extinguisher and pulled the pin, but I couldn't get it to work, so I threw it down. My galvanized water bucket had smashed together and I grabbed that and pulled the sides back apart. I got up on the washboard and started bailing water into her. Fire licked around my bottled gas, so I threw a bucket of water on that. I got the flames above deck, but with the rocking of the boat, fire sloshed back and forth under the deck and I couldn't get to that. That surge was setting her back afire as she rocked one way and the other. I looked to the stern deck. A blaze of fire was coming out.

By that time other crabbers were all coming to me, but scared to come aboard, thinking she might blow again. I had that propane tank on there for the little gas cooker I kept in the cabin. The cookstove blew overboard, but that tank stayed bolted down.

Darius Horsman got to me first and said, Jump overboard! Leave her!

I said, Can't do it. Just throw me your fire extinguishers—got to try and get this fire out.

He threw me two extinguishers and pulled on off to let somebody else alongside. They didn't want to lay by me, but passed near enough to throw me their extinguishers. When I wasn't using them, I was using my bucket. Every once in a while, I swiped my bucket down into the water and lost my footing on the washboard. My feet flew up in the air and overboard I splashed again. I pulled myself back aboard and, when the next man came by, I got another bucket off him and two more extinguishers. Before I got all the fire out, I used twenty-eight fire extinguishers and four water buckets. I wasn't gonna leave a brand new 32-foot boat. After I got the fire down, two or three of the guys come to me and jumped aboard to help me bail the water back out.

Daddy was running his trotline on the other side of Fishing Bay when all this started, so he wasn't that far from me. We were still bailing out water when he reached us. I had gotten enough water into her to smother the fire out against the deck. We were bailing the water back out when Daddy pulled alongside. He was right glad to see me.

***

That day on the boat, I was wearing a National Guard field jacket and my left sleeve was gone from that. My arm got burned some and my hair singed off. Other than that, I just had a bad cut on my hand. Everybody thought I ought to go to the hospital and get checked up anyway, so Darius took me to the Island and my brother-in-law Steve Gray drove me to Cambridge. They put five stitches in my hand, where I still have a scar, but I can't say anything about that. The emergency room doctor explained how I might have inhaled that flash and died. My engine box cover saved me. The force of the explosion took the easiest way up. My floorboards were weighted down with twelve or fifteen barrels of crabs, so the blast came up through the engine box, blowing this half-inch tongue-and-groove lid off. That heavy cover blew up in the air and come down looking normal. As far as you could see, it had just turned around in the air and landed intact, but if you pushed on its top paint skin, your finger went right on through. It was nothing but ash. That cover had shielded me from the ball of flame and absorbed the blast that would have killed me if I'd inhaled.

***

Probably Daddy was remembering a time I blew up the old gas stove we had at home. That day he'd laid down on the couch in the living room. I was gonna warm something in the oven. I turned on the gas, then went around the house looking for a match. When I found one and stuck it in there, she blew me up against the far wall of the kitchen and rolled Daddy right off the couch in the living room.

What happened? he asked when he got up and came to the doorway.

Standing there, my white sweatshirt burned brown, I didn't have to do too much explaining.

I blowed the stove up, I told him

***

After the boat explosion, Daddy towed her and my catch to Bernard Murphy's at Farm Creek. I'd lost at least six hundred pounds, maybe eight. All my basket crabs had blown overboard. The barrels hadn't blown out, but the top crabs were red. When they dumped the barrels into Bernard Murphy's steamer, running lights fell out, and a frying pan— all that stuff that had blown up in the air. I still had 1,306 pounds of crabs Daddy landed for me, then he towed my boat back to his little railway at Shorters Wharf.

An explosion like that will usually split the bow of a boat, but hers didn't open. If I'd thought quicker, I should have pulled a plank off and sunk her instead of fighting that fire. It wasn't real, real deep there. That's the onliest thing I would do different, but I never thought of it quick enough.

When she blew, Brice Hurley sat on the Island in his outdoor toilet. He heard that Varrooom.

He told me later, I didn't know what that sound was— guessed one of those jets from Patuxent broke the sound barrier.

Wallace Morris, a veteran, was looking right at me when she blew. He said, You went straight up in the air. Your boat looked just like a battleship I once saw burning.

Things could have been a whole lot worse. Louella's brother Steve was the lucky man, 'cause he was going crabbing with me that trip. I went to pick him up off Poplar Island, but he'd overslept or something. When he didn't show up, I went on back out in the river. And I'm thankful it didn't blow when Henry Jones gave me that jump. It might have drownded him. He hadn't pulled many yards off. And I was lucky the engine lid was on, so I didn't get killed inhaling the flash-burn. As it was, that night had been cool enough that I still had my field jacket protecting my arm. I was extra red in the face and my hair singed, but after flying out of the boat with all those crabs and windows and everything, I just had the one cut on my finger.

That same month, a crab-potting boat blew up out in Chesapeake Bay off Hoopers Island. One fellow drowned and another got picked up from hanging on a gas can. They'd had a mess of gasoline aboard, about seven cans. Their gas pump tore up and they were feeding gas by pouring it when the engine backfired.

One lesson I learned from my accident: when you're going out mornings, open the cabin door and go in there and see if you smell fumes. If you smell any gas at all, don't start her; she'll blow. I know that's the closest I ever come to leaving here.

I never got back to crabbing that year, but everybody came from everywhere to Daddy's railway and helped me get her back together. They came with hammers and nails and got her done in a couple weeks. When oystering came in the first of October, I was ready.

Chapter 14

JOINING THE GUARD

That field jacket I had on when my boat exploded was from the National Guard. I don't know why I'd joined the Guard, except I was seventeen at the time and it was more or less something to do. It wasn't like in Daddy's time. Daddy never had no choice about going in the service. He got drafted into the army and sent onto the beach at Normandy—not in the first wave, when the National Guard got all cut up, but those first guys were still in the water. His unit swam ashore through blood. Like most veterans back home after getting shot at and beat and banged up, he never talked much about it. I do know he walked across France into Germany. He was a scout with the Second Cavalry Reconnaissance Troop. After the breakout from the beach at Normandy, he went out on patrol. He and another guy stumbled onto a crowd of Germans in a bunker. I believe his buddy got killed, Daddy shot in the shoulder. That winter he got frostbite, walking across Europe in the snow.

***

When I decided to sign up in the Guard, my cousin Elihu was already a buck sergeant in Company K in Cambridge, moving up quick. His brother Ted joined about the same time as me, then Jimmy signed up for a few months before going regular army. We were part of the 115th Infantry and had a good platoon. We all stuck together. When someone wanted to go out some night, he went and others covered for him. We had the reputation as a platoon of screw-ups, but they called on us when they wanted a job done.

We had different officers from around the state come sometimes and they all knew Elihu. In the guard, they called him Sam.

When the star general came through he'd ask, Where's Sam Abbott at?...Sam, what have you got to tell us?

Elihu had a fine mind for poetry. Anything he heard one time, it lay on his mind, just like it was stamped there. Traveling away in the trucks for training, he shortened the road for us calling out verses. One year he'd tell you a poem, and twenty years later he could tell it again, never dropping a word out of place.

***

I got out of the Guard in the 1960s, after all the troubles in Cambridge, but before that, the Guard was all right. We had meetings in Cambridge every Monday night, and exercises in the summer at different bases. I was in reconnaissance and got assigned to a tank, one of four guys in that thing. At different times I was the loader, or

Master Sergeant Elihu Abbott

gunner, or driver, then I made tank commander. Every spare minute, we had to be working on her: changing oil, cleaning her up, her breaking down, Somebody leaves the hatch open to look at something and here it comes—another tank ahead or anywhere close throwing mud all over you. Boy, I wouldn't want to go to war in one of them sumsabitches.

***

When we set off for training, we always had a trash can full of beer and bottles in the truck. One summer to Indian Gap, Pennsylvania we rode down a road so rough I got sick. I stuck my head out of the truck, and threw up all over a platoon sergeant standing by the road, his swagger stick tucked under his arm.

One year we trained at Fort A. P. Hill, Virginia, another at Fort Bragg, North Carolina, attached to the 83rd Armored Division as a support outfit. I was driving the tank one day when we were only supposed to be going firing, but we ended up on a tank range. I was following another guy and saw him go through a tank trap full of water.

I said to the boys, If he can go through there, we can go through there.

I squeezed right up in a knot and put my foot to the floorboard, just hoping to see daylight again. We came out the other side, but the hatch was left open. I got so muddy they had to send me back to the barracks in a jeep to change clothes.

By the time I got transferred out of tanks, I was proud to be a rifleman.

***

Down south another time, we bivouacked in the woods in tents. Out on patrol, we came up on this farmhouse out in the middle of nowhere—an old guy sitting on the porch in a swing. We were hot and thirsty as the devil. A fence stood all around the yard and I went inside the gate.

The old guy stood up and said, That's far enough.

I said, Buddy, we're operating here with the Army National Guard. You got anything we can have to drink?

He said, All we got is half-and-half.

We got luckier another day. We rode up in the hills and came to a four-way crossing. Two guys in a car stopped the other way at the same time.

We hollered over, Hey buddy, where can we get some good moonshine?

Shaking his head, the driver said, Dunno. There ain't none 'round here.

We started to pull off, but they must have talked it over, 'cause he hollered, Hey boys, hold up. We might be able to help y'all. How much ya want?

We said, Two or three gallons.

He pulled over to the side of the road, got out, and flipped his seat back. They had two compartments under there. They'd been sitting on four gallons in each well, eight gallons altogether.

I said, Is this good stuff?

He said, This is *good* stuff.

We bought four gallons, carried them back, and put them in the base refrigerator. The 'shine was clear white and looked just like cold water, but a glass of that would turn you on. By suppertime all the cooks were knocked out and nobody else could figure out where we had the 'shine hidden.

Somehow or other, in the PX one night we got in a fight with an airborne unit. Our mess sergeant was this big, strong guy from Cambridge, so I got behind him.

I said, I'll cover your back, Sarge.

He was knocking one guy into two others, bowling them over three at a time, when I spotted the MPs coming and said, Sarge, we gotta beat it.

Me and the sarge jumped out an open window and got away, but all the rest got busted.

***

Jimmy didn't stay a year in Company K before going

regular army, ending up in Germany. I stayed eight years in the Guard—wouldn't have gotten out then except for getting called up for duty every time I turned around. I kind of hated to leave the Guard, but couldn't afford to take off work so often. The Guard barely paid a dollar a day When our pay got

Company K in 1967

raised to $1.50 a day, I thought we were really doing something They only sent a check every three months, so our pay would look bigger. The biggest check I ever got was around $30, which came in handy in those days. On the other hand, I remember one time the Guard called us up to Cambridge about the fifth of October, just when oystering opened up. In those days, oysters were what we depended on to carry us through the year. Right at the first of the season was the best of it. I could land thirty-five or forty bushels a day. At four dollars a bushel, that came to $150 a day in early October, a hundred times what the Guard paid. Crabbing was just a sideline at that time.

***

If it wasn't Cambridge, it was Ocean City. In March 1962, near the end of muskrat season, the governor sent the

Guard to Ocean City to stop some looting after a bad nor'easter they called The Ash Wednesday Storm.

We hadn't had much wind around home, nothing near sixty mile-an-hour like they had on the ocean side. I didn't know nothing about how bad it was over there, or about us being activated. I'd been to town and was driving home in this old '51 Chevy I'd bought from my Aunt Helen. When I got to the marsh past Hurleys Neck, tide was coming on quick. I always carried a .22 rifle with me, so I started shooting muskrats that swam in that rising tide. I just had on my regular clothes, but I waded out collecting them—the water cold, but not real cold, considering it was still muskrat season.

By the time I worked down to Old Ditch, about a mile above the Island, everything was all the way underwater except me and that Chevy. I'd just shot another muskrat and was wading after it, tide up above my waist, when I heard a plane. I looked up and here came a seaplane circling lower and lower. He looked like he was gonna pitch right on top of me, but he set down alongside Old Ditch

The pilot glided up close, cut the engine, and yelled over to me, Man, is there something wrong? You need some help here?

He'd seen me wading around with nothing but water all around and thought I'd got stranded out there in a bay or something.

I said, No, nothing's wrong.

He says, You know the tide's rising?

Yeah, I said, I know it's rising. I'm on my way home right now—leaving as soon as I get this muskrat.

Everybody says a car won't run with the tailpipe under water, but I know one that did. She sounded like a wet exhaust on a boat, glub-blub-blubing. When I got hold of that last muskrat and waded back to the road, water lay up onto her seat. I thought I better not stay no longer or I might not make it. I expected her to conk out any minute going through that last cut before the Island bridge, but she ran right on up onto the Island and down to the house.

When I went in Louella said, The Guard called for you to report to the armory and go to Ocean City.

Well, I said, I can't drive nowhere now.

I took my little aluminum boat and went back muksrating around Poplar Island. All together, I shot fifty-two muskrats, some along the road from the car, then more from the boat.

***

By the time that tide ran off and I reported to the armory, my unit had already been two or three days in Ocean City. Trucks shuttled back and forth and I rode one of them from Cambridge to the oceanside. That storm had been the worst nor'easter in a century. All of Assateague Island had gone under. Waves twenty-some feet high came in, rolling right over Assateague and carrying dunes into city streets. Sand lay six feet deep and had to be hauled out of town in dump trucks. My unit patrolled West Ocean City, so those private homes and trailers across from the city wouldn't get looted. The bad stuff happened uptown and everybody'd been evacuated. Before the Guard got there, looters took anything and everything from stores The guardsmen probably had more liquor and beer in their bags than regular people, but they didn't bother other things. My unit stayed outside the city about a week, patrolling west of the bridge in eight hour shifts, carrying M1 30.06 army rifles and no bullets.

Chapter 15

THE TROUBLES

We didn't have no bullets all those times we got called to Cambridge either. I thought I'd had it one night up there. I felt mad anyway, 'cause I'd been called out so often. By then, I had young'uns at home and couldn't afford to lose so much money. The troubles in Cambridge lasted years, off and on, with demonstrations and counter-demonstrations and white night-riders racing up and down Pine Street. It looked like the Wild West sometimes. At one point, Elihu came and told us we'd been federalized. It got nasty, especially when buses rolled in with out-of-towners. That's when the big troubles started.

George Wallace from Alabama came to the old skating rink one night to make a speech. A counter-march came down Washington Street to Peachblossom. We expected a bad clash that night, but nothing much broke out. They got Wallace back out of town as quick as they could.

Usually the trouble started at night. The rest of the time we mostly just laid around. A lot of guys slipped out— me for one—usually to Johnny Riggin's place out on the highway. They had music and everything going there. It got so bad, the first sergeant had to hold roll call every two hours to see how many he'd lost. Right after roll call, we took off. An hour or two later, sitting in Johnny's, I'd looked up to see big old Sergeant Newcomb coming in with three or four others.

I'd say, Boys, we've had it.

The sergeant would just say, Come on, boys. We gotta go back to the armory now.

He wasn't mad or nothing. He knew where we were. We'd get up and go.

I got called so often I started slipping home to work whenever nothing was going on. By the time the first sergeant found me gone, I was gone again.

After getting me back once, the sergeant said, I'll fix you this time, Abbott. I'm putting you on that deuce-and-a-half truck leaving for Havre de Grace.

Units from other parts of the state got called to Cambridge sometimes, so trucks hauled tents and cots and stuff. When this truck got ready to leave for Havre de Grace, I put somebody else on there in my place and I went back home again. It took two days before the first sergeant missed me that time. They got the marine police out looking for me.

They kept us till things quieted down, then let us go home. After a couple days at home, trouble sprang back up and the Guard called again. We slept on cots at the armory. When they had to add units from other parts of the state, those guys had to sleep in pup tents at the high school.

This one time the Guard called for me, the marine police came and told me to go to Cambridge for a riot. I had my car parked at Farm Creek. I tied my boat up and drove from there to Cambridge, stopping at every beer joint in between—five or six at that time. When I parked at the armory and got myself to those big, steep steps out front, I couldn't climb them. Elihu saw me coming, taking one step forward and two back. He knew I was loaded. He came and got me by the arm real quick, took me in the basement, and started shooting coffee in me.

About eleven o'clock that night, a demonstration turned ugly. It had been building up all day, but I didn't know that when I drove to town. Coming from Farm Creek, I passed right through where all the trouble started without noticing nothing. I didn't have my uniform on yet and I just sailed along. After Elihu got me on my feet, my unit was called on another fire. My squad followed Rescue Fire Company trucks whenever they made a run. The firemen were all volunteers, not even getting a dollar a day like we did. We were all getting pelted with stones and things and hearing rumors of snipers. Luckily the sniper rumors were mostly false, but we didn't know that then. We jumped in the back of this deuce-and-a-half truck and away we rolled from the armory, following the fire call to Washington Street, right back where I'd come from. There was a crowd gathered on the corner of Washington and Race Streets. Besides locals, busloads of demonstrators had come from up north and all over. I was still half-drunk when we piled out of the tailgate. I ran about

Wylie (left) and fellow-guardsman in their "steel pots"

twenty feet, fell on my face, and I bet a dozen Freedom Riders ran across my back.

I always hated that steel pot you had to wear on your head all the time, but I appreciated it that night. Everything in the world rattled off of us, stones and beer bottles and brickbats. All the guardsmen were worried, expecting sniping. We were under the command of a colonel who'd just got in from Baltimore a few days before. Those out-of-town battalion commanders who came over here didn't stay long. They might stay a week, then line her back where they came from.

This latest colonel stood up in his Jeep with a bullhorn saying, Please go home. . .please go home.

Up above him, a second-floor window started coming up real slow. I spotted it and pointed my rifle up there. The window slowly came back down. Somebody up there had something in mind. We didn't have neither-nothing in our rifles, but next time we got called back on riot duty I carried my own ammunition from home.

About three hundred head of demonstrators gathered there, some sitting in the intersection by Haddaway's filling station, knotted up in a pile. They wouldn't leave, so we started pulling arms and legs to sort them out. They were stuck together like crabs in a basket.

We weren't getting anywhere fast, so we hollered, Hey, we need a little more help over here.

The Crisfield guardsmen were with us, a transportation unit, mostly black. They felt mad as we did about being called out, 'cause they made good money in Crisfield too at that time of year. Instead, they were stuck in Cambridge, hauling demonstrators off for a dollar a day.

Those Crisfielders said, Give him here.

They started sorting out arms and legs. One black Guardsmen said, Cut the mother loose on three.

He counted as they swung the first guy, One. . . two. . .three.

At that, they let him fly, bouncing him into the truck.

About that time a brickbat came flying and struck the colonel. He tumbled out of his Jeep into the street. I thought he was killed, but he popped back up.

All right boys, he barked, shoot the tear gas to 'em.

We had gas masks and I fumbled around trying to put mine on, standing there with my rifle between my legs, huffing and puffing to blow my mask clear of gas. I couldn't get it to tighten up. I think I got more tear gas than either demonstrator. All at once, something hit me on the shoulder.

I spun around and found that colonel, patting me and saying, You're doing a fine job, Soldier.

After that night, I'd had enough. When my enlistment was up, I got out of the National Guard. Oystering was in season and trapping starting soon. No end of demonstrations was in sight and I couldn't afford to lose any more money.

***

I can understand demonstrating for your rights, but there was no need for that violence. Big cities or other places might've been different, but I thought people in this area were pretty tight together already. I know I sold many a muskrat along Pine Street, where Rap Brown called for fires to be set. I used to go door-to-door there selling muskrat meat.

A black woman there said something one time, calling me a white man.

Her neighbor said, That ain't no white man. That's a red man.

Another Pine Streeter got the best of me one day when I knocked on her door, asking if she wanted to buy any muskrat meats.

Will they keep? she asked.

Yeah, they'll keep good, I said.

Then keep 'em.

***

But then in the early 1960s things got so stirred up, gunshots were fired and one policeman shot. It's a wonder nobody got killed. For my part, I know I never wanted to hurt nobody.

Chapter 16

THE VIENNA CANVASBACK AND 'RAT CLUB

When I settled on Elliotts Island in 1959, besides working on the water and joining the National Guard, I got a job as a hunting guide. When I was growing up, Daddy took care of that six hundred acre property called Jobes Point for a gunning club, but he wasn't much for duck hunting himself. He was more interested in trapping their marsh. In return for that, he took care of the members' lodge and their boats and built boardwalks all over the marsh for them. As we boys grew, we helped him build and brush blinds with reeds to camouflage them, keep the boardwalks repaired, chores like that. We got wood and, when the members were coming down, started a fire for them.

Before going back to the city one Sunday, a club member named Mr. Veazey said, Wylie, I'm coming over duckin' next weekend. If it's all right with your Dad, I'll swing by and pick you up to go with me.

I said, I'd like that, Mr. Veazey, but I ain't got nothin' to shoot.

Don't worry, he said. I'll bring something you can use, and enough shells for both of us. Tell your mother I'll bring your dinner too, so she doesn't need to fix anything.

After that, he used to drive down every Saturday from the western shore to go ducking. He was an ex-navy man who didn't have any sons of his own, so he took me along for company. He came to the house before daylight, bringing our food and everything we'd need out on the marsh that day. For me to shoot he brought a double-barrel .16-gauge shotgun.

We drove to Jobes Point and took one of the club's boats down the creek to a blind on Bullocks Pond. We killed a lot of ducks on that pond, shooting all day long. Or if we didn't get any, that was all right too. Either way, we never came in before sundown.

I was only about ten and I thought something of Mr. Veazey, picking me up at my door and delivering me back home—letting me use his shotgun every week. He'd been way up in the navy in the war. Finally, he got married and only lived a little while more after that. His wife got everything he had, including the shotgun I thought I might end up with, but I'd learned a lot about ducking.

***

Before I ever moved to Elliotts Island, a handful of big-money sportsmen had bought up most of the marsh above the Island and built themselves clubhouses. Dittle Hughes from Hurleys Neck guided for one club that had a lodge alongside Elliott Island Road on Pokata Creek. In the late 1950s, other executives came along from Wilmington and bought an old Hurleys Neck house that had been in Dittle's family. For marsh to hunt, they paid $40,000 for six hundred acres on the Nanticoke River.

I was skinning a raccoon one day behind Dittle's clubhouse when a couple men pulled up to talk to him. They saw what I was doing.

What are you gonna do with that 'coon? one asked me.

I don't know, I said. You want him?

I do, he said. We're having a game dinner.

I must have said the right thing, and probably Dittle put in a good word for me. They turned out to be members of the new club and they needed a local guide. I was nineteen, not long over from Robbins, but they must have thought I filled the bill. I got hired.

***

To reach my club's marsh, we had to run down the Nanticoke River. In ducking season, I moved my workboat from the Island harbor up the Nanticoke into Wapermander Creek, which ran nearly to the clubhouse. Harboring there for the season, whenever we went out ducking, we only had a short drive to get aboard with our gear. I could carry up to ten head aboard *Miss Wendy*, the name I gave my workboat after my daughter was born.

To the beginning of our marsh, I had about a ten minute run down the creek to the mouth of Wapermander, and maybe another ten minutes to go about a mile down river. Before the fall season started, I set up blinds on the river shore and on creeks that ran off into our marsh. Where I set up, I cut marsh grass and brushed a portable frame to make it invisible, then set up a board for a seat. We could set those portable blinds anywhere, in the marsh if we were gonna shoot black ducks, or along the river for canvasbacks. We didn't use regular stationary blinds till it got real cold.

The first river blind was usually just below our property line, then another on Long Point. Farther down, we had one on the point at Jacks Creek, which ran up into our marsh and branched into Steeleyard Creek and other little creeks and guts. We had our own names for a lot of spots, like Canvasback Point, where we had a good day, or Slim Pickins where we didn't.

At one time I had thirteen members in my club. I'd scatter them out, two or three to a blind on the riverbank, others in the marsh. Canvasbacks were the big thing when you could kill four or five legally. There was no better place for canvasback than ours. We tried to get each member a couple days gunning for canvasback on the river and a couple days in the marsh.

Members used to rag me about my speed, said I only had two speeds, wide open and dead stop. To tow our decoys, we put them in wooden skiffs Powell Horsman had made at his boatyard at Henrys Crossroads—just above Hurleys Neck on the Island road. Zigzagging down the creek one day, I rounded a bend too fast towing the skiffs and sunk them both with the whole rig aboard. Years ago I could tow them down once and leave decoys in the skiffs all season in the creek behind the blinds. People didn't steal stuff like they do now. Whenever we went out, decoys waited right there ready to be set out without my dragging them back and forth. As time passed, it got harder and harder to hang on to decoys, even under lock and key.

***

I hunted to the point at Jacks Creek one day with a member who didn't know me very well yet. We had a canvasback rig set up and we sat in the blind waiting for ducks. He kept looking at my gun.

Tell me something, he said. How do you camouflage your gun that color?

Ain't nothing to it, I told him. All you gotta do is keep her in the boat two or three nights and leave her and she's all camouflaged.

When I first married, I'd got that Winchester pump, Model 12, seven shell. I bought it for forty dollars off a guy over Tedious Creek who'd seen somebody with an automatic and didn't want the pump anymore. Man, I killed some ducks and geese with her. She's a collector's model now, but I lost her when somebody busted in Smitty's gun shop in Eldorado, where I was having her worked on.

***

Some of those boys took pride in their high-priced guns—and their dogs, too. They brought down $3,000 Labradors that ran the marsh so fast, they ran right over the ducks they were supposed to retrieve. Those expensive Labs were mostly field trial dogs—one a five time champion. But gunning over seven-foot sage, a field trial dog's useless. They're used to looking for hand-signals instead of using their nose. My Chesapeake, Leroy, was the best I ever saw. When people had a bird down and couldn't find it, they came to the house to borrow Leroy. He'd work for anybody, the same as for me.

I got Leroy from a guy in Talbot County who trained dogs for field trials. He tried to make a field trial dog out of Leroy, but Leroy didn't qualify, maybe because he knew more than the guy giving hand signals. Anyway, the guy couldn't do anything with Leroy and didn't want him.

One day I was up there and he asked me, You want this dog?

Yeah, I'll take him, I said.

That was a lucky day for me. The first day I carried Leroy in the marsh, we went shooting on the Nanticoke River. His first retrieve, he brought the duck to the shore, dropped it on the bank, and came up to me walking real slow. I knew then somebody had beat the hell out of him. I didn't say nothing. By the second week he came out of all that stuff and we never lost another bird after that.

***

Some of the club was gunning for ducks one day when these geese came over, so I said, Okay, we'll get a couple geese.

They knocked down two that hit the water and went straight for the marsh. I knew they were wounded and they'd get up on that marsh and hide in the grass. The tide ran awful strong, so I took Leroy in the boat and allowed about fifty yards for the tide, then went over against the bank. Leroy went up and brought one back to me.

I said, Go on there after the other one.

He went back and in a couple minutes I heard him barking. He came to the boat with no goose, but he had a feather hanging out of his mouth. I thought to myself, he knows where that goose is, but it's hung up some kinda way. He took off hard as he could go, then he came back and looked at me. I laid the boat against the bank and got out. He took off, then stopped and waited, looking back at me like to say, I know where he's at. He led me to this big, crippled goose hung up in waterbushes so thick he hadn't been able to get it out.

Gunning along the river, I needed a good dog. When a cripple went down and the tide wasn't too strong, I sent Leroy and followed in my skiff. Leroy's head would be scanning from side to side like radar, then suddenly he'd catch the scent and take off up the bank into the marsh. Watching a good dog work is better than shooting.

***

One day I showed my gunners a trick I'd picked up from an old-timer. I carried a bunch of club members down and put them out by the blind.

You gonna put the decoys out? one asked me.

I told him no.

Whadda you mean?

I told them, You all get in the blind while I get everything straight.

They knew I was up to something. I put the big boat away down the creek and walked out on the marsh with a shovel in my hand.

What are you gonna do with a darn shovel? one asked

I'm gonna put out my decoys, I told him.

I cut myself four or five nice round shapes out of the mud with that shovel and set them up. Before I got the fourth one set, ducks were coming in. We killed twenty-some ducks of all nationality that day using what the old-timers called tumps.

One gunner said, I've seen every damn thing in the world, but I never seen decoys made out of mud.

***

When it blew southwest, the river could be a rough sail after we rounded Long Point, heading for the creeks that run into our marsh. Above Long Point, only seven hundred yards of marsh separated the Nanticoke from Bozes Ditch, which ran through our place off Steeleyard Creek. I decided to blast a shortcut. Lev Davenport helped me, along with a man who worked for the county. Lev owned a lot of timberland and all the marsh around Cokeland in Hurleys Neck. We put two sticks of dynamite every eighteen inches across that seven hundred yards of marsh, from the river to the ditch. Then we waited back on the other side of the creek with a plunger for high water, so it would give us more vim. When the tide raised up to the top of the bank, we pushed the plunger and everything took off. Muskrat and bull turkle and fish flew through the air. We blew a canal ditch seven hundred feet long, deep enough I could go through there in a wooden skiff. That cut ten minutes off our sail and meant we didn't have to run down river below Long Point when it was rough. Now you can take a workboat through the canal ditch.

Chapter 17

THE POTOMAC RIVER

There was something going on over to the Potomac River when we all had to start oystering away from home in 1962. We worked hard and we played hard over there.

Jimmy was home the first of the season. We tried working home in Fishing Bay, but couldn't get more than twelve bushels between Dad, Jimmy and me.

Me and Jimmy told Dad, This ain't hardly nothin' now and they're still dyin'. We hear there's plenty oysters in the Potomac. Come on go with us and we'll try 'em over there.

Daddy said, I'll go, but I'm driving my car 'round there. If I don't like it, I'm comin' back home.

That began five years of oystering over there, when all the oysters around home died off. Me and Jimmy sailed *Miss Wendy* over to meet Dad. As I came into Cobb Island harbor my first time, going around this buy-boat, I ran *Miss Wendy* into the corner of that big old market boat. I punched a hole into my boat about two feet above the waterline. Dad met us and found a guy with a piece of plyboard and patched her up for me.

We three slept in the cabin of the boat at Cobb Island, which didn't leave very much quarters on there. We found nobody much staying around Cobb Island, so we went over to Aqua Land Marina and harbored there, where Route 301 crosses the Potomac. Where we tied up, a restaurant stood off one side of the boat and a bar off the other. Me and Jimmy were steady going every night, and we didn't have to move around far.

We came back one morning about three o'clock. Enough light showed around there that we could see Daddy looking up from his berth, none too pleased with us.

Where you two been?

We just been over here to the beer joint, I said pointing over my shoulder.

Well, he said, if you're gonna do this every night I'm goin' home.

Daddy didn't travel to barrooms. I don't remember a time he did. I know if he'd ever carried us boys into one, my mother would've killed him.

About the third night me and Jimmy came in late, he got disgusted with us and went home. When the weather got cold, I found a room at the motel and stayed on tonging.

***

Another year I took Newton Ruark over with me—an older guy from Bishops Head. We went over after ducking finished in the fall and he culled for me.

A few days after we got there Newton said, Wylie honey, I don't know why you rent a room. You never use it.

I said, I never know when I might want a rest.

Well, Newton said, I know you just do it to help me out. If it wasn't for me, neither bed would ever get messed up.

All those little towns over there had bars and hillbilly joints, and Route 301 around Waldorf had a string of big casinos with slot machines—a lot different from what we were used to at home. The guys would leave the Eastern Shore Sunday evening and get over there around half past eight. Uptown at a hillbilly place in Waldorf, Sunday nights at nine or ten o'clock was about the time it started rolling.

I sat at the end of the bar there one night cutting up a little bit with this girl. The guy next to me leaned over, talking low.

He said, She's lesbian.

I thought he said, She's Liz'beth.

I just misunderstood him. By the time I oystered on the Potomac, I knew what that meant, but growing up down Robbins we didn't know nothing about that.

During the week, we'd come in from oystering, take a shower and sleep two or three hours—all we needed. Then we took off and went to town. We stayed out all night four nights a week.

***

We stayed in nice motels over there and only paid something like $12.50 a week. We checked in Sundays and left Friday nights. Between the slots and our card games, some of the boys worked all week, then didn't have any money left to carry home. They had to borrow gas money to get to the Eastern Shore. I always kept $150, big money back in the '60s. I had three little kids by then and didn't want anybody fussing with me.

All the money didn't come back across the Bay, though. We were in the Stardust Inn one night, me and this other boy. I got a dollar in quarters from the bartender and went over to the machines. The fourth quarter I put in there, I won $75 and spent it all right there, setting everybody up.

Wendy, Wylie Jr., and Robert aboard Miss Wendy *on a family picnic at Duck Island in 1969.*

I sat in the Stardust another night with a buddy, listening to the band. Between songs, something came over the loudspeaker about this friend of ours and some Waldorf girl getting engaged.

I said to my buddy, Did you hear the same thing I did?

Yeah I did, he said. How's he gonna get married to two women at the same time?

That friend of ours was already married back home here.

***

One year I stayed at the Thunderbird, along with some brothers from down below. One of them had new teeth that kept falling out on him, so he went uptown in LaPlata and got some glue to hold them. He used too much glue sticking them in, then he couldn't get them back out. He sat on the corner of the bed while his one brother and another boy wrestled those teeth. Finally, they hooked their fingers in there and got his teeth out of him.

I was at the other end of the room shucking oysters. Those oysters were so fat it didn't take many to make up a gallon. I brought ten gallons back with me when I came home and made good money off of them. Shucking in the motel, I had the room fixed up so it wouldn't make a mess. I'd carry the shells and throw them in the woods out back. It wasn't nasty or nothing and by the time they got on to us, we'd scattered out of town anyway.

***

I hardly ever had a fist fight in my life—not like Jimmy. I had one, though, that started with some locals in that hillbilly joint in Waldorf. I was by myself that night, sitting at the bar. I saw a guy ask a girl to dance. When they got on the floor, I could tell he wasn't what she thought she was getting. I went out on the floor and tapped the Groper on the back.

I asked her, You wanna dance?

She said, Yeah.

This was near closing time, when we had our dance. I finished my drink and walked on out the door. I didn't see him at first and he didn't say nothing when I came out, but the Groper was waiting. First I knew of him, he swung at me. He never touched my skin, but his hand whiffed by and struck into my collar. I already didn't think much of him and hell flew into me then. I swung back and struck him, knocked him down, and jumped on him. I landed right on top and was putting it into him, when here comes two more Waldorf boys. Well, a couple boys from home, Ronnie and Joe, happened to see these guys were gonna gang up on me.

They came over to the Groper's buddies and said, Boys, that's far enough. You better stay right here.

I let up on the Groper and he and his pals took off. Joe and Ronnie and me went and got in our own cars. I had my new '66 Mustang at the time. I was driving on down Route 5 when those three pulled up along side, ran me off the road, and pulled over in front of me. I was bull-headed enough, I got out and walked up to where they'd stopped. About that time, another car pulled in behind mine, which I thought must be a cop. I went to the driver's window, found the Groper there, and reached in to grab hold of him.

He said, What did you hit me with a while ago?

This tall guy walking up on the passenger side said, Tell him you hit him with an Eastern Shore sumbitch.

When I heard that, I knew it was Joe and Robbie who'd pulled in behind me. They'd seen these guys take off and thought they were setting me up to follow me. Joe and Ronnie followed them. Now Robbie stood at the passenger window.

Why don't you haul your asses out of that car? he asked.

When he said that, they took off. I still had my arm crooked inside the car, holding the Groper's shirt. My windbreaker caught on the window latch and I had a time getting loose. That guy towed me down the shoulder of the road. I was lucky to keep on my feet, running till I could bounce out of there when he slacked up to pull back onto the road. He spun his wheels, throwing big old stones on me from alongside the road. I thought sure my windshield would break, but it didn't.

I never got in many fights. You near about had to hit me to get me started, like the Groper got me going that night. They might've done me in if Joe and Ronnie hadn't come along. That was gonna get nasty.

The last time I went to that Waldorf joint, four or five of us took a taxi up there from Aqua Land, but there was nothing left.

One of the guys said, Damn if it didn't get hot here last night. The place burned down.

***

The dancingest people I ever saw in my life lived in Colonial Beach, Virginia. I was in my element when I went there. They nearly danced the feet off of me. Maryland owned the whole river, so slot machines stayed legal right up to the tide line on the Virginia shore. A pier with dancing and gambling reached from there out into the Potomac. If somebody got out of line, they got locked in a room out on the pier till the Maryland police got there to carry them away.

Another rough place was at Indian Head, near a military base. I went up there one night.

One of the sailors in there said, You got no right to be in here. This is strictly a military place.

Not knowing better, before I ordered anything, I asked the man behind the bar, Is this strictly military here?

Who told you that?

I pointed, That man there.

The bartender went over and snatched that guy up and threw him out of the bar. Another night, I saw a fight in there. They had the drill down so good, before the song on the jukebox finished, they had everything put right again. When the song ended, there were no more fists flying and nothing on the floor. They'd broke up the fight, straightened the tables and chairs, and mopped the floor.

***

We usually harbored at Aqua Land. Inside there, they had a barroom, with rows and rows of slot machines. The jukebox had a screen on top that showed pictures, like the music videos they have nowadays, only tamer. Past that you came to a dining room, and behind that, a room for private parties where we played cards. I don't remember there ever being any trouble there, but we liked to look around the territory.

Some of the boys would have a car over there and a bunch of us would pile in and go different places. Two or three of us went into Leonardtown one night. Walking into this one place, they had swinging doors like you see in movies. The girl who come over to wait on us had long net stockings all up her legs.

I told her, Honey, them things you got on there, they'd gill a bull minnow.

If a gal was big, we might tease her saying, You look just like the *Fannie Insley* lying stern-to.

Fannie Insley was Cap'n Raymond Evans' big old schooner. She'd lost her shape, but she used to haul seed oysters to Fishing Bay, when private beds like Joe Gray's grew right up out of the water in a good year—the best-tasting oysters around Chesapeake Bay.

Chapter 18

THE OUTDOOR SHOW

All those years growing up, and on up till today, I always look forward to February and the Outdoor Show. Back in the late 1940s, all muskrat season my father lugged big bundles of 'rats home to the garage every afternoon. After walking the marsh all day fishing 'rats from his traps, moving traps, and resetting them, his work had just started. In those days, everybody stretched the hides after skinning their catch. Every house had rows and rows of nails lining the attic, where hides hung on stretcher-boards drying out. We boys would be out there in the garage every night till way after dark doing what we could to help Daddy.

Skinning every evening, day in and day out, I got to be a pretty fast skinner. I was ten years old the first time I skinned against a stopwatch. Me and my brothers were on the roadside fooling with our own traps we worked after school, when Baker Robbins drove past. Baker Robbins dealt in fur and owned and rented thousands of acres of marsh to trappers. He stopped his car this winter day and began backing up to where we walked with our little mess of 'rats we'd caught.

Looking at Jimmy and Doug, I said, Wonder what Mr. Baker wants.

When he got back to us he asked, Boys, how fast are you skinnin' a muskrat? Can you skin one a minute?

I said, We don't know, Sir. We'll go home to practice and see.

Daddy and his brother-in-law, Herbert North, trapped together that year. They brought their whole load of muskrats back to Daddy's garage. We messed around helping to skin and put the hides on stretchers, but we never worked up a lather at it. After talking with Mr. Baker, we did some serious practicing, skinning and timing each other for three or four days. It took some strength to cut on the hide and pop the 'rat loose, but we wrestled with them. When all three of us could skin a 'rat in a minute, we went down to Mr. Baker's cannery as hard as we could go.

Mr. Baker, we got it! We got it!

Da'gummit, get down here and show me, he said. If you qualify, you're all in the show.

That meant the Outdoor Show that he and Emmett Andrews and Fred Malkus started back in the 1930s. We got down on the floor, each boy with a 'rat, and Mr. Baker took out his watch.

Okay, boys, he explained, I'm gonna say ready, set, and then when I say Go, you take off skinnin' hard as you can.

When he said Go, we started cutting and twisting and tearing at our 'rats. Maybe he cut us some slack, I don't know, but before he hit his stopwatch, we finished.

Boys, he said, you're all in.

We'd all qualified with a one-minute-'rat. That first time skinning against a stopwatch, I was ten, so Jimmy was nine and Doug was eight. We skinned in the 1950 show with our cousin, Ted Abbott. His brother Elihu, being ten years older than me and Ted, skinned against grown men. Elihu won World Champion Muskrat Skinner his first time in 1953. I won five times as a junior skinner between 1950 and 1957, when Junior North beat me, then in 1958 we graduated to the men's competition.

***

There was something for everybody in those old shows. Parts of the show looked like stupid-people-tricks they do on television nowadays. All kinds of characters played parts.

Charlie Willey broke brickbats over his head. Uncle Herbert's father, George North, and Curtis Insley from Cains Ditch skinned blindfolded. George North imitated things around the marsh, too, like he could do the sound of a whole pond full of bullfrogs. He won the 1938 contest, the first time they kept a record of speed-skinning.

I always carried an extra 'rat for my Uncle Parks in his later years. I knew he'd be looking for me when I got to the show.

Sam Kenney (left) and Parks Abbott competed in an exhibition match.

He'd say, You gonna give me a 'rat so I can skin him out?

He got on stage skinning that one 'rat while the rest of us skinned five.

***

Our cousin Elihu could do anything he put his mind to. Taxidermy was one of the things he picked up. Elihu figured out how he could skin a 'rat making just two cuts, where we'd always made a lot more. Skinning by his new method, Elihu punched the hide out, sort of like he was turning a sock inside-out.

He came out to Daddy's garage and showed us boys, his brother Ted and me and my brothers. Jimmy didn't pick it up. Jimmy kept on skinning the old way. Either way, to start, we speed-skinners got down on one knee, with five 'rats lined up according to the order we wanted to tackle them. When the timer said go, we took up the first in our row. Jimmy would pick up one leg of his 'rat and cut around that, then pick up its second leg and cut around. He won the title doing that in 1966, but when we started using the new technique, by the time he sawed around a couple legs, I was halfway through my whole 'rat. All serious speed-skinners use Elihu's two-cut technique now.

Elihu started competing in 1952, before he'd invented two-cut speed-skinning. He finished way back in the pack, but got a new knife and a five dollar bill for being in the show. After that he got serious about competing and won eight World Champion Muskrat Skinning titles. Trappers came from different places to skin against us. A trapper from Louisiana came up here and saw Elihu's technique. He went back home and taught them down there. Gary Schroeder from Pennsylvania won in 1966. Robert Mudd came up from Louisiana and tied me for first place in 1977, but Jay Miller from Cameron Parish, Louisiana was

Elihu Abbott before the 1982 Outdoor Show.

the fastest. He beat me out for the title four times in the 1970s. If he'd ever won three years in a row, he would have gotten to keep the big permanent trophy. He won two in a row twice, but never put three together.

***

Cameron Parish holds the Louisiana Fur and Wildlife

Festival every year. Their pageant queen and a team of speed-skinners travel every year to our Outdoor Show, then they invite our show's winners to their festival. I got to be good friends with Benny Welch, a school principal who was Louisiana state skinner.

Benny came up every year with his family and we hung out together. He'd walk my marsh with me. Down south they trap mostly from their boats and don't have to walk. Our marsh is a lot different from theirs.

Walking the Pound Marsh with me one time, Benny was pulling his boot out of a hole and told me, This is tough going. In Cameron Parish, our marsh is all level and flat.

This'll make a man out of you, I told him. I used to rib him saying, What you've got to do is get some oyster tongs going and build up some muscles.

A man's got to have strong hands to skin 'rats. By the time a skinner's on his fifth 'rat, he's putting all his energy into it. I really think tonging helped a lot to get me in shape.

***

If Benny thought I skittered over that marsh good, he should've seen my brother Doug. Dougie could walk marsh the lightest of anybody I ever saw in my life. I had him on my marsh one winter. I set traps up while he fished others. I sent him out to fish twenty-five and looked over my shoulder and there he was, right back behind me.

I said, Doug, there's another one over yonder.

He said, I got that one. I got all these in here you told me.

First time I doubted him a little bit and said, You sure you fished 'em?

I looked around and he'd fished them.

***

Those boys from down south brought their own 'rats up with them. 'Rats are easier to skin the fresher they are, so they kept those Louisiana 'rats alive till the contest. Checking into the Quality Court in Cambridge, they carried them to their rooms—eight or ten to a garbage bag—and dumped them out in their bathtubs.

Benny said, You should see those maids run out of there when they find those 'rats swimming around in the tub.

Before I got to know the Louisiana boys, me and my son Willie got to the contest one night and started walking across the parking lot. Two guys were running around a car. Benny was one, but I didn't know him.

I said to him, What's wrong?

He said, We lost one of our 'rats. The darn thing got out of the bag.

He sounded southern and I asked, Who are you boys?

We come here for the Outdoor Show from Loosiana, he said.

We were gonna help, but about that time the second guy caught the 'rat and put it back in his bag. I don't know how they could reach in a bag with those 'rats. They could reach down and pick them up and feed them. I went to pick one up and he like to eat me up. I had to skin with a bad cut finger.

What each of their skinners did back then, he carried his bag of 'rats out onto the stage. He reached in and took out a 'rat and struck it across the nose to kill it. Then he laid that one down where he was gonna skin and took out another, till he had five lined up.

The Humane Society got after them and they had to quit bringing live 'rats on stage after a night when the blow didn't kill this one. The 'rat jumped up and got loose on the stage, running under the curtain. A muskrat's faster than a streak of lightning. Contestants backstage for the beauty pageant were screaming.

***

We use Conibear traps, setting them underwater in leads on a low tide. A Conibear kills instantly. I decided to experiment saving some muskrats once and live-trapped a couple. The garage was too cold for them, so I put them in the bathtub in a cage. I know Louella wasn't too happy, but she didn't say nothing.

It was interesting to sit there and watch them. Those two 'rats stayed in their own corners, then they'd come to the center and hit each other, then back into the corner again so quick you couldn't hardly see them. You had to have your eye right on them or you missed it. They fought like that for two days, till we were due for a cold spell. I went in there that morning and they were cuddled up. They knew that cold was coming. That's the way they live in a muskrat bed to create heat. Outside they'll freeze to death, and it doesn't have to be real cold either.

Anyway, after the night that 'rat ran away across the stage, they made a rule that all muskrats have to be dead at least two hours before show time, and they have to be killed somewhere off-property.

***

Fresh or not, their southern 'rats are always easier to skin. Louisiana 'rats don't have the fat on them that ours have up here farther north.

One day, waiting backstage, this Cajun skinner told me, I've got an extra 'rat if you want to try him.

I skinned it there backstage and it popped right out.

As Elihu said, Those Louisiana 'rats peel like bananas.

***

On stage getting ready for the skinning, the announcer always tells the audience that there can't be any flashbulb cameras going off. There's too many sharp knives slicing and clicking around up there. Nobody needs to be blinded by a flashbulb. Skinners do enough bleeding up there anyway, rushing and slipping up accidentally.

Actually, we skin as much by feel and memory as by sight. Somebody like Elihu could do it blindfolded. Eyesight figures into it some, though. I found that out when Willie got into the men's competition in 1984. He became my main competition and beat me a time or two. Then I tried wearing glasses on stage and took the title back for a little while.

***

My son Robert probably could have been the fastest of us all if he'd taken it seriously. In 1984 we finished one, two, three—me, then Willie, then Robert. My daughter Wendy's won the women's title and so has my daughter-in-law Pam, Willie's wife.

My aim was always to skin five 'rats in under a minute. I've done it in practice, but never set that official record in the show.

Benny Welch told me, You could skin five of our 'rats in way less than a minute. You never would lose if you had

Robert, Wylie Sr., Wylie Jr. and Wendy Abbott with Outdoor Show trophies in February 1983.

our 'rats.

I had the five-in-a-minute record set one year in the show till I lost a 'rat. What happened, picking up one 'rat, I accidentally hit another and knocked it out of line. Then I jumped over to the third 'rat and forgot to come back and look for the second. When I finished, I only had four hides.

I asked the guy next to me, You don't have an extra 'rat over there, do you?

No, he said, I just got five.

When I got up, my missing 'rat was under my leg, and I'd skinned four in forty-some seconds. That night I'd have skinned five in under a minute easy, because you generally get in a rhythm and pick up speed as you go.

Another year in the early 1980s I came within 1/100 of a second of skinning five in a minute. That year I accidentally flipped a couple and had to turn them back over to make my first cut, which cost me time.

***

A lot of guys get penalized so many seconds for messing up around the head, but I could sling them out. When it got around the head and eyes, others would be sawing on him, and that's where I could beat them. I used a 313 Buck knife. Most everybody used the same kind, either the 313 or one called an Old-Timers, which is just like a 313 but with a little more back on it, which I don't like. I like a perfectly smooth blade.

In Vernon Boog's fur house, where he bought hides in Vienna, some people came in once and wanted to see me skin a muskrat. I put two on the floor and skinned them in sixteen seconds—eight seconds apiece. They said they wouldn't believe it if they weren't looking at it. That's when I was right; I was in my heyday then.

***

Out on the marsh muskrating, more often than not

you're on your own. I'm right at home out there, but to someone not used to it, marsh is a lonesome-looking place. Muskrat season runs from January to the middle of March, through the worst freeze-ups and snowing and blowing. If you don't watch the weather and you get caught out there, trapping can get dangerous. Every so often a man doesn't come home. Then all the other trappers go tracking him, afraid of what we're going to find.

We didn't go out in rain or snow if we could help it. A job like my youngest son Cory's got now with the government trapping program, they go out in snow or when snow's laying on the marsh. That ain't good. Somebody's gonna get hurt going across and breaking through ice, when they can't see where they are. We always waited till the time was right to fish our traps, when we were naturally supposed to be out there trapping.

The first time I helped look for a trapper, it was Jimmy Stewart who hadn't come home. I was around fourteen, going along with Daddy across old Mr. Jimmy's piece of marsh. Around midnight, a couple black ducks jumped up in front of Daddy. When he threw his light on them, there lay Mr. Jimmy. He didn't have a muskrat on him, so he must have had a heart attack as soon as he got out there. Another time, when we found Pete Robbins, he had nine in the pockets of his muskrating coat. Ice broke through with Pete. You don't want to trust ice in February.

Like most trappers, I've trapped every winter since I was a boy, alone more often than not. But one weekend a year trappers get a chance to all get together and play at their job. That's the National Outdoor Show.

$\mathcal{C}$hapter 19

LOUISIANA

When I won my skinning titles, I won an invitation to go down to the Louisiana Fur Festival in Cameron Parish. The first year I went down there, I'd never flown before. I was scared to death going aboard the plane at BWI airport. The girl on the plane had miniatures.

I said, Give me two of them.

That was before we took off.

Then when I got to Louisiana, they put me in a helicopter with our Outdoor Show queen and the Louisiana Fur Festival queen. We had to go to Beaumont, Texas airport to meet the fur queen coming down from Canada. I thought

A float in the Cameron, Louisiana Fur Festival parade shows a Cajun band playing at a bayou hunting camp.

to myself, this is all right, me sitting among three queens right off the bat, but I had my doubts about this chopper pilot.

On the way to Beaumont, we choppered out to see an

offshore oil rig. This pilot was flying along steering with the stick between his legs. Every so often, he'd rear back laughing. I never said a word, but I had to wonder why he let out such big laughs. Something was going through his mind. The oil rig looked like a little speck in all that water, but he hit it okay.

When we got to Beaumont, he set her down in a cow pasture.

The queen's plane hadn't come, so the pilot said, You want to go in and have coffee with me?

We put the chopper away and went to the restaurant.

Sitting there over coffee, I asked, How long you been flying these things?

He said, Well, I been flying her for 9,000 flying hours.

I said, All right, I'm not gonna worry about it no more.

***

My friend Benny Welch met me in Cameron Parish and took me all around. He trapped mostly from his boat, but the Louisiana marsh I saw was all nice and hard for walking. All our marsh around home isn't such sucking mud as folks complain of who're not used to it. Part of our marsh is hard like theirs—so hard old-time Islanders grazed their cattle on it. Alligators are the big difference between our marsh and theirs. In Louisiana, you can see alligators crossing in front of you at the same time as cows out grazing. I thought maybe those alligators would eat the cows up, but they didn't.

Alligators lay fifteen or twenty eggs when they nest up. Those guys take some of the eggs—not all—and hatch them out and raise them. The most chance of getting bit is in the mating season. One like to knocked Benny out of his boat when he got up next to her nest of eggs.

Benny has an alligator farm. They grow eight or ten feet long. The guys down there were really making out off nutria then, getting ten dollars for fur, then feeding the rest to their gators. Those guys had a market for nutria fur when we didn't, even though our fur's thicker. I'd go out with them down there shooting nutria when I went to the festival. Benny sent me T-shirts and some alligator meat after I came home.

***

Those folks around Cameron Parish have a big time at their festival. There's parties, banquets, a parade, and a skinning contest. I couldn't get in their contest because I already had the world champion title, but they had me do an exhibition.

The sheriff of Cameron Parish called me up on the stage and gave me a gold key saying, This key will open up anything—anyplace you want to go for the next three days.

Saturday morning about ten o'clock, this guy pulled up in his Cadillac to pick me up and be my driver. We rode downtown and saw this skeet-shooting match going on. There was no skeet-shooting around home then and I never had shot any before. Shooting ducks is all I did back here. I could shoot well enough, but I wasn't no pro at it.

I said, I believe I could shoot some of them.

My driver said, You wanna try it?

I said, Yeah, I'll try it.

He backed up and went over and said something to this guy and come back.

Come on, he said.

They gave me a shotgun and twenty-five shells. They turned them clays loose somewhere and they came by. I busted twenty-three of them.

Me and the guy rode around all day in his big old Cadillac to every legion hall and bar. I couldn't spend a cent. They wouldn't take one penny from me. We had the finest seafood—every kind. A platter would have gator tails, loads of shrimp, crawfish. Crawfish are good, but there's too much picking, which I guess is how others feel about our crabs.

Everything down there was spicy and there was lots of rice.

***

Nobody never heard of a cell phone then, but this guy driving me had a radio phone in his Cadillac.

I called home and Louella said, Where you at?

I'm in downtown Cameron Parish, sitting riding down the street in a Cadillac, I told her. She didn't believe me, but that wasn't nothing. In the parade I rode down the street on a horse. Horse riding was something else I never did in my life, but I knew how to steer him—pull to the left or right on the lines going to his jaw to turn him, or pull back and he stops. The guy I'd been traveling around with held the horse and helped me get on, then he walked alongside of me. He had two or three jugs of Jack Daniels hanging out the saddle bags, and I was already drunk before I got on.

One old woman got hold of the deputy sheriff and said, There's a man drunk here on a horse.

The deputy told her, He's all right. Don't worry about him.

***

The Budweiser Clydesdales horses came for the festival parade. They've got the prettiest hooves on them. And during the whole episode, these old Cajun boys rode up and down the streets pulling wagons with bands on them. They rode a block or so, then pull over and cut loose playing. They stayed awhile, got people dancing in the street, then moved on somewhere else. I liked to hear that music and did some Cajun dancing different places. I used to dance anything—ain't nothing to it, just get your rhythm and follow the type of music, whatever it is.

***

Me and Willie went together one year with a bunch of people from around Vienna. This one old gal liked her beer, plus she'd never flown. We got a six-pack for the drive to

BWI airport. While we waited for our flight, she wanted a hot dog and another beer. This was about nine o'clock in the morning. When our flight was called and we got to the gate to board our plane, she didn't have her ticket. Willie ran through the airport like O. J. Simpson, fetching her ticket from the lunch counter. They held our flight till he got back. First thing after we got in the air, she had to go to the bathroom.

I said, Go in the back. There's a bathroom back there.

I heard some clanking and looked over my shoulder, and she was beating on the exit, trying to open the hatch.

I said, *No honey, not that door.* You pull that one and we're all gone.

Festival day in Cameron, the Vienna crew all went in a store and bought beer, but doubted drinking in the street was allowed. When they got to the parade, they found guys wearing hats with hoses that ran beer down into their mouths. Empty cans and bottles were piled up everywhere.

***

One trip I got drunker than hell and passed out in the bed in my motel. When I woke up I found my buddy there on the other side of the bed.

I said, We gotta go. The show'll be starting.

He said, It's over with.

Whenever Benny came up to our Outdoor Show, we used to take off together. Sometimes the folks there worried we weren't gonna make it back for the main event, but we always did.

Chapter 20

MIDDLEMEN

Bernard Murphy ran the upper crabhouse at Farm Creek. Daddy and me and Jimmy dealt with him all the first years I worked on the water. Bernard was around Daddy's age—a good man. He had one room overhead of the whole building where he kept everything for boats and motors. Anything we needed like alternators, starters, we didn't have to go to town. He had them right there and sold at good wholesale prices. He looked out for his crabbers. You couldn't beat Bernard Murphy. I got to working other places, though, and dealt with other buyers not so fair.

A lot of times crabbers buy their gasoline and bait from the same dealer they sell to. In a bad season, they might get too far behind. Some old-timers would crab all season to come out of the hole. I've never done that bad, but I've sold crabs for as little as five-cents a pound. I got tired of some of the greedier middlemen wanting it all. I started hauling crabs myself, first to Cambridge, then to Baltimore. Later I went everywhere in the world to sell crabs—New York, New Jersey.

Early in the 1970s, I carried my crabs and a few of the other boys' to the old Cambridge ice plant. There I met a guy who bought and hauled them to Baltimore. As fall came on, in the Choptank we caught a lot of sooks—female crabs. Off Cooks Point one day I caught sixty-seven bushels in five hours. Brice Hurley was with me in *Miss Wendy* culling them—sixty baskets of sookies and seven baskets of number ones. I had them stacked up and lost some that rolled overboard off the stern when it got rough down there on us. The buyer paid us $2.50 a basket for sooks. One day I was at the icehouse with a buddy of mine, Lindy Pritchett.

The buyer told us, I don't know what I'm gonna do. There's no market for all these sooks. I've got six or seven good crabbers and don't know how to get rid of some of 'em.

Me and Lindy looked at each other, then said, Here's two you don't have to worry 'bout. You can eliminate us.

***

Lindy was a dude—a tall, skinny guy with curly, wavy hair. He was born down below at Bishops Head, but you could drop Lindy anywhere and he'd make out all right. We set up to meet at eleven o'clock the next morning to go to New York and try to get some orders.

We started buying sooks and hauling them to New York in this 6-wheel truck I got. In Cambridge, we had no market for them at $2.50 a basket, but we could buy them right to the dock there and haul a truckload to New York, where we got $10 or $12 a basket. Sooks is what they wanted in New York. I still had my regular pickup, too, so I bought males and sent them to Baltimore in the smaller truck with my brother-in-law. Me and Lindy each went out in the river, catching crabs and buying more off other crabbers, then loaded my 6-wheel Chevy, and hauled to New York. It's no wonder I ran off Elliotts Island Road so much, falling asleep on my way home nights.

***

Those boys up there in the city told me the first time I went up there with crabs, Keep two on your truck when you come up. Bring a second driver or they'll steal truck and all.

When I drove a big order to Baltimore myself, old Brice Hurley used to go up with me. Coming home, we'd stop at a fast-food place in Glen Burnie, me with a load of money on me, two or three thousand dollars if not more. All these trampy-looking guys walked from place to place around there and I thought to myself, Boy, I'm gonna get robbed. Mugging wasn't as bad at that time as now, but it's a wonder

I didn't get knocked in the head.

When I was gonna haul to Baltimore, I met my crabbers as they came in and loaded my pickup and drove over the Bay Bridge. After deliveries, I never got back out of the city before midnight. Driving alone once about one o'clock in the morning, I got pulled over speeding. The trooper probably figured I'd been drinking, but I hadn't had neither one. He could see a six-pack on my floor though, and wanted to run me in. He tried to find a trial magistrate, but couldn't find neither one to take me to. I hadn't said nothing up to then. I saw he was gonna turn me loose.

He said, Get off the highway when you come to the next exit.

I said, All right—first exit, I'll get some sleep.

Route 10 was getting put through after the tunnel and I thought to myself, I'll pull over here and park. I pulled in and dozed off with the motor running. I woke up feeling something around the truck. I raised up to look out the window and a face stared back at me, nose to nose, with an Afro big as a bushel basket. He scared the living daylights out of me. I couldn't get away fast enough. That's the only time I ever got bothered up there.

***

I got myself in all kinds of scrapes trying to avoid middlemen. It's a wonder I didn't get killed or kill myself. I wasn't a hog, though, like some. One crabber I did business with went down south of the Carolinas and ran about two thousand crab-pots overboard. I think the folks down there nearly killed him. He had a boat blow up on him and, last I heard, was talking about going to another country.

***

I thought me and Lindy landed in another country first time we got to the Fulton Fish Market in New York. The people around there weren't regular Americans. First day we carried crabs up there, we backed up to the loading dock and started putting our baskets out. This gang stood out there on the dock, giving us the look. Every man of them held a big hook by the handle, or had one hanging over his shoulder.

The guy we'd sold to saw us and came running, saying, No, no.

I said, What's up? This is your order.

You don't know, he said, glancing back at the crew with all the hooks. You no unload your truck. That's their job. You do it, you take money from them. You no wanna take money from them.

After that we hired those guys and never touched the baskets, but another guy from Cambridge lost his truck there.

What we didn't sell at the market, we tried going down to Chinatown, restaurant to restaurant. First place we pulled in, there was a pair of ducks hanging up just like they flew in there—feathers and head and everything. The guys in the market stalls we could understand a little bit, but we couldn't understand them at all down to Chinatown.

Man, there was something going on there evenings around seven or eight o'clock, and it went on like that till the next day. I was right down there in the heart of it all selling sooks. The Chinese call them cow crabs. We only did that once, through. We found out that territory belonged to somebody else too, and we didn't want to step on nobody's feet. You step on somebody's feet, they might put you out of business.

***

One day I delivered at the Fulton Fish Market, where I'd come to have four or five big dealers I sold to regular. One of the guys who had a stall there, I don't know what he was, but he wasn't American. After paying for the crabs he took me aside.

He said, How 'bout haulin' some cigarettes along with

crabs next trip?

I told him, I ain't haulin' no gawddam cigarettes.

When it started getting like that, I got out of there. I didn't like the way things were heading, but Lindy didn't care. He set up a seafood business in New Jersey and settled there. He came back home to visit sometimes, but spent most of his time up north. He made a lot of money but he died young of a heart attack. I think he worked himself to death.

***

Me and my buddy Grant Barnett, another trapper, carried fur up there in the '70s, too, to sell not far from Fulton Street. We watched the fur market going up and down and did all right, selling at the right time. I stood there while the buyer culled them out. He said he expected to ship our furs to Germany.

Then we went to New Jersey to see Lindy Pritchett. We had $10,000. Grant took a hundred and I took a hundred, and we left the rest in a coffee can at Lindy's seafood place before getting in his Cadillac to go to lunch.

Grant Barnett with a fox he trapped.

After lunch, Lindy said, Let's go drink one beer.

I said, Man, we gotta get home.

Why don't you stay up here tonight? he said. You'll be fresh to go early tomorrow morning.

Me and Grant had been out all night for two or three days before leaving home, so we agreed on staying. Next we stopped at a go-go joint. We drank one beer and left there. We went about two blocks and to another go-go joint. We started back to Lindy's after three or four places like that in Jersey, but he changed his mind.

Hell, he said, let's go into New York. . .just a little while.

I said, I don't care where you go. You're driving.

We started on Lancy Street and ended up on Broadway. In the bar on Broadway, this girl sat there on a nearby stool.

We told the bartender, Give that girl there a drink too. . .How much we owe you?

Eighty bucks, he said—regular beer twenty dollars a bottle.

I said, Grant, we better get out of here.

No, no, he said. We won't go yet.

I said, If we stay much longer, we won't get back.

So we went back to Lindy's in Jersey, where he had cots. We slept there and got up the next morning, got our stash, and come on home. On the way out, we went a couple blocks and saw a muskrat bed. They had 'rats right there—a lot of them.

***

I drove up to New Jersey again with Joe Hughes one day carrying about thirty baskets of crabs on the truck. I had a friend who'd moved up to New Jersey from Elliotts Island years before. I met up with him and he rode around with us looking for markets. We stopped one place and went in this restaurant.

I asked the guy in the dining room, You handle any crabs here?

Do we handle crabs! he said. We handle a pretty good load of 'em.

Who owns this place?

That man there with the pot of potatoes, he said pointing. You gotta go to the kitchen to talk to him. Go 'round back and you'll get hold of him there.

We struck off around the corner of the building, thinking we'd unload all our crabs right there at that one stop.

I asked this man, Do you use any crabs here?

Do we use any crabs! I'd say we use crabs.

How much can you use a week?

I can sell six or seven baskets.

So we set off again. Finally I wound up in Vineland, New Jersey. I could see the lights of Atlantic City from Vineland, where I found a good market with a guy in a restaurant there. I wanted to keep that man there happy.

He called my house early one fall morning, saying, I need fifty baskets. Can you take care of me today?

I'll fix you up, I said.

I went straight to Hoopers Island to those crab-potters and got fifty baskets of big, black crabs. Man, I felt proud of them. I helped basket them; I loaded them. Two and a half hours later, I pulled up in Vineland. I couldn't wait to show off. I lifted a basket lid for the man and half of the crabs had died. He took them anyway and didn't say nothing, but that's how quick they can die, especially if they're not caught trotlining.

Then, going back home through Vineland, I got a speeding ticket.

***

I was lucky in Maryland, though, hauling crabs to Baltimore. I didn't get but two warnings. The first one, a state trooper pulled me over on Route 50 in Easton for speeding.

He came up to the window and said, Let me see your driver's license and registration.

He looked at my license and said, You that muskrat skinner down to Cambridge?

Yeah, Officer.

Oh hell, he said, go on.

I was working as a pipefitter one fall at Duponts in Seaford when I got stopped the second time. I still hauled late crabs to Baltimore, then I came back across the Bay Bridge and cut through Hurlock to get to Seaford. I figured I'd work at the plant till the weather warmed up. The town cop in Hurlock let me off with a warning too.

I nearly got killed, though, before I got out of that plant. They put me down in this hole on a lower level while a crane lowered some heavy machinery. I could move quick in those days. I heard the chain slipping on that crane and got to the stairs before the big crash. A gang stood around the railing on the upper level looking down watching.

One guy said, Oh my gawd! Where's that little man down below?

I said, I'm right here behind you.

Grant worked there at Dupont's in the off-season, too. He had a line of traps set on the back lot of the plant that he fished during the day.

***

For about a two year stretch, I ran off the marsh road every week—more often from falling asleep or trying to get home too fast, but sometimes from being all drunked up. Some nights I was lucky if I landed in the ditch. One night Sherwood Moore always liked to rag me about, my truck was so far off in the reeds he just could see the roof when he went by the next morning.

There's a bad turn by Savannah Lake I never even tried to round another night. I flew off straight ahead and slept the rest of the night there. About daylight, Earl and Sharon Hurley came down to go crabbing and I hopped up on my roof and waved them down.

Freddie Harrison crabbed for me and he always came down to the Island early. I had to hustle to get back from Baltimore to give crabbers like him their fresh baskets before they started out mornings. Hurrying this one morning, I landed my 6-wheeler in a pond near Savannah Lake. I seldom got caught anywhere without boots, but that time I just had my good shoes I'd worn to Baltimore. When I saw Freddie's headlights coming, I flashed mine and waved him down. He pulled up on the turn I'd missed.

Well, Gator, you done it again, he shouted over to me.

Yeah, I hollered from the cab. You got your boots with you?

Freddie said, Yeah. Why?

You gotta come get me. I ain't got no boots.

Freddie put on his boots from the back of his truck and came on out to me. I crawled out my window and got on top the cab. Freddie turned around and I climbed on his back. He carried me piggyback out to the road. I thought we'd both slip face-down in the mud, but we made it.

I had to replace my crabbers' baskets, so I asked Freddie, How 'bout goin' back and gettin' the baskets off the truck? You guys are gonna need them.

Freddie turned around, waded back across the pond to my truck, and got out my new baskets I'd need to give the guys down to the wharf. Then he drove me home to get out of my good shoes and into my waders.

Bill Harrison kept a small wrecker at the Upper Store. By the time I got dropped there, he already knew my truck was in the marsh.

Come on, said Bill. We'll go up there and pull her out.

We called him Bulldog for good reason. Bill latched on and yanked on her, snatched on her, did everything. My truck sat at such at a tilt, I was afraid she'd go over, but about ten o'clock, an electric company truck happened along. They hooked their winch to the down side of my truck and held it so it wouldn't go over while Bulldog pulled her out.

Chapter 21

ISLAND DUCKING

Beside hunting clubs with lodges up on the marsh, come fall a lot of ducking went on right off Elliotts Island itself. Five or six off-shore blinds ringed the Island in the 1960s. When I moved on there, Bill Chew had his Duck Inn on the point, near the foot of the Island road. He and his guests hunted an off-shore blind. At the upper end of the Island, some guys from Baltimore built a little shack they called Pancake Lodge behind 'King David' Gray's house, just across the bridge by the Upper Creek. They had an off-shore blind there. I put together a rig to build blinds and drove down pilings and built off-shore blinds all around the county. Around home I built a couple between the two clubs' blinds on the Island's north shore, one off Red Hill, another below that, off my in-laws' place.

Besides my gunning club up the road in Hurleys Neck, four or five gunners from Wilmington stayed with my in-laws, Joe and Helen Gray. I kept the blind back there for them and carried them out when my own guys weren't down.

Most all of these guys had big executive jobs. The ones who stayed with my in-laws had top jobs at Remington Arms and Hercules Powder. Others gunning around there owned race tracks or were government scientists, lawyers and such. They brought one of Franklin Roosevelt's sons down once with a couple of his boys.

***

One morning early, I went up the road and ran into a couple gunners from my own club who'd come down looking to go out on our marsh.

I said, Okay, we'll go see if we can get a couple ducks.

Before we left the clubhouse for my boat, two carloads of federal game wardens passed by, trailing boats down the road towards the Island.

I told my guys, We don't want to go out today. It's gonna be too hot around here.

My guys weren't hogs, but you never know how fairly you'll be treated if you get checked over. We didn't need the hassle, so I left them and turned around to come back home. Driving through the Island, I didn't see any wardens anywhere till I went down to the Lower Creek. Down there at the harbor, two uniformed drivers were hanging around their cars, the boats still on their trailers. That meant those drivers must have scattered wardens around afoot, surveilling the Island.

Sure enough, two had gotten out at the Upper Creek and snuck back into the bushes on the point to watch the Pancake Lodge bunch from across the creek. Three gunners were in their off-shore blind, banging the devil out of ducks. My neighbor Gib helped out their club some. I saw his pickup parked outside the Upper Store, so I found him and told him what was up.

I said, You go get 'em out of there up to King David's and I'll go down and get these other boys out down home.

Gib went across the Island bridge for the Pancake Lodge boys. Meanwhile, I went to the guys in my blind down to my in-laws' and waved them in. Those guys down home weren't doing nothing wrong, but the Pancake Lodgers were shooting three or four ducks, then running their skiff ashore with those ducks, putting them on the marsh, and going back out for more. They thought they had their ducks hid, but the wardens crouched there in the reeds just watching. No telling how long they'd have watched ducks falling, but they saw Gib drive up and wave those guys in, so they radioed for their cars. By the time the Pancake Lodge boys saw Gib and got ashore, the government cars rolled in, penning them up in their lane. The gunners got fined $450 apiece.

Those wardens wanted to arrest Gib in the worst way, but didn't have anything to charge him with. Maybe they should have been satisfied with writing all those fines and not have more ducks shot.

Those two from my own Wilmington club who'd come down never got to go ducking at all that day, but at least they weren't out nothing but gas money.

***

Some game wardens wanted me, too, in the worst way. I started duck hunting near about as soon as I got old enough to climb out of bed and never had a charge against me till the early '90s. They charged me one December 11th. I could have paid a $200 fine, but I got bullheaded because I hadn't done nothing. Two state wardens, DNR cops, charged me with shooting over bait and I didn't even have a gun with me.

I had three guys out on public marsh off Jacks Creek, two sons of club members and a friend of theirs. Two had come up from Texas and one from Louisiana to go ducking. The club had a rule against non-members hunting their marsh, so I carried them to state marsh where it joins up to ours. We went in my fiberglass T-Craft and set out the decoys, then I went up this little gut waiting in the boat while they shot.

We hadn't been there but fifteen or twenty minutes when two state wardens pulled up. I was nearly half a mile from the gunners. The wardens went on by the gut where I was sitting without seeing me, but I could watch them. They checked my gunners' licenses and checked their bag limit and checked for lead shot. Everything was fine. They started walking for their boat, then one stopped and turned around.

How'd you get down here, he asked.

Wylie brought us down here, this one guy said.

It was like lighting a match then. If that boy hadn't said I'd carried them, the wardens would have gone on out, but of course the boy didn't know no better. When I saw the cops coming towards me, I stood up in the boat. I knew them both. They pulled up alongside, talking just as nice as can be, then the one in the middle seat got up and come up on the front seat.

Wylie, we got a problem, he said.

What kinda problem we got? I asked him, because we were allowed to be hunting on state property.

He said, We were here eleven days ago and found feed up here.

So I asked him, Why didn't you post it?

He didn't answer me on that, because if they find bait on state property, they're supposed to post it, No hunting for so many days in that area. The one running the motor started talking to me and the one up front jumped out into my boat.

The one staying in their boat said, We found feed here.

I asked again, Why didn't you do something about it then?

No more than twenty seconds passed since the guy jumped in my boat. I looked and he had a handful of little grains of milo.

I said, Where'd you find that at?

Right here in this boat, he said.

I never used that boat feeding ducks, so I said, I'll be damned if you did. You never found that in my boat.

Well, he said, go get your men and pull your decoys up and meet me in Vienna in an hour.

We did like he said and waited about another hour at the Shell station in Vienna before they come along with another car in back of them carrying a federal warden from Fish and Wildlife. They knew they didn't have enough to convict me, so they went and got the federal man. It's a different story when the federal gets into it. Then it gets blown all out of proportion.

The federal man said, What's goin' on?

I said, Man, I don't know. We were out there huntin' on public land and these two guys came along and said we were shooting over bait.

He said, Were you?

I said, No, I wasn't shootin' over no bait.

Which I wasn't. They just wanted me so bad, and they'd never got me, so this is what they done.

The federal man said, Wylie, tell you what. I can give you a ticket and fine and we'll go on.

He was gonna write me a ticket for $200 and I wouldn't take it. I was going to court. My three guys from down south had to take their tickets or else fly back months later to stand trial.

Three or four months later I got papers in the mail, United States of America vs. Wylie Abbott. That'll hurt a veteran's feelings. Then I started making trips to Baltimore. Man, that's another world. One trip I had to go get my fingers stamped and a mug shot taken at the U. S. Marshall's office. Another trip I had to go get fingerprinted again somewhere else.

The first trial date, the state was there but the federal wasn't there, so they said, We can't have this trial today 'cause our witness isn't here.

The whole day was shot, and the federal guy hadn't never seen nothing noway. All he did was meet us in Vienna. That first trip, they had me charged with shooting over bait. I wasn't hunting and didn't even have a gun there. Next time they reduced the charge to aiding and abetting.

This was spring and we were fishing, but I had to keep taking off. I stayed overnight at my lawyer Sam Kenney's house so we could be in court in the morning. We got this old retired judge on loan from New York who'd never been hunting. He didn't know what a duck was or what a marsh was or a boat or anything else. Everything the Natural Resource man said, he believed.

He asked me one time, You mean he's lying?

I said, Yes Sir.

There's no doubt in my mind the federal man knew they were lying, too. He never said nothing. I know what they did. That man had milo in his pocket when he jumped in my boat. I never saw no evidence after he put that milo in a plastic bag and got out of the boat that day, but me and Willie counted out something like what he'd held in his hand. He held at least three hundred grains of milo. He'd have to be a vacuum cleaner to pick up three hundred grains of milo in twenty seconds.

Sam did as good any anybody could have with that judge, but federal charges blow everything out of proportion. The judge fined me $1,200 for aiding and abetting, six times what the hunters paid. If I'd got caught in the wrong, I wouldn't say nothing about the fine, but I went in that court clean and came out looking like a stuffed rabbit.

Chapter 22

SOME DOGS OF MINE

Leroy, my Chesapeake Bay Retriever, had a nose on him—the best I ever saw. I was out in the marsh one day in the early '60s, cutting pine branches to cover a river blind. Leroy dived into a hole under a hollow tree, tunneling in so far, only his hind feet stuck out.

I called, Leroy. . .Leroy, come on, let's go.

He didn't move. He just stayed in that hole, till I thought he must be stuck. I had my axe, but I didn't want to take a chance on hitting him. I went around to the other side of the tree's trunk and bent down chopping and chopping. Before I got through with my axe, I heard scrambling and looked up to see Leroy running down the beach after a raccoon.

Another day, as we crossed the marsh, he stopped dead and started digging like mad. I thought he'd gone crazy. Then he broke through to a muskrat lead with a teal hunkered down inside.

Hunting nutria, Leroy had the knack of grabbing a nutria by the back of the neck without getting himself bit. If you saw him

Wylie and friend home in the garage from the marsh.

shaking and killing some nutria, you'd think he'd tear up a

duck, but he didn't. He had a mouth so soft, he could retrieve an egg.

***

Those gunners of mine paid a lot of money for field trial dogs they brought down with them.

They went on all the time, Oh, what a nose my dog's got.

What I'd do, I'd hold Leroy back and give those gunners a chance to hunt their dogs. After they gave up, I sent Leroy. One day shooting teal up the creek, they had a Black Lab running the marsh forty miles-an-hour.

I said, He's running too fast. He's running right over top of the ducks.

The Lab would come back and the guy'd send him out again. Me and Leroy just sat there till finally they gave up.

Then I said, Fetch 'im up, Leroy.

If my dog couldn't get 'im, the gunner said, *he's* not gonna get 'im.

Leroy went across the marsh and, two or three minutes later, came back with the duck.

Gawddam, the fella said, I don't believe that.

***

A bunch of us sat around up to the clubhouse one evening—Leroy dozing in his spot by the tin stove, other dogs lying here and there. The gunners were all talking to each other: my dog can do this and my dog can do that. A new guy bragged on his champion Lab and what a nose he had.

I listened awhile, then I said, Ol' Leroy here has a pretty good nose on him, too.

That stinkin' thing? he said.

Leroy lifted his head and looked at me. They all went on bragging.

Finally I said, I'll tell you what. I bet if I throw this

pocket knife of mine as far as I can out there in the dark, ol' Leroy will bring it back.

The newcomer bet me five dollars it couldn't be done. We all went out on the porch and I sailed that knife into a field of sage across the road. I sent Leroy and he was gone and gone.

The gunner said, You're out five dollars, and a pocket knife as well.

Finally Leroy came back and the guy said, He's given up.

I knew Leroy wouldn't do that. I put my hand down, Leroy opened his mouth, and out came the knife.

The gunner said, That's just luck. I bet he can't do it again.

I knew it would be easier the second time, 'cause the scent would be all over it. We won an easy ten dollars that night. Next day, we went ducking and the gunner's champion Labrador wouldn't go in the water.

Ol' Leroy won me some money. I could throw a quarter out in the marsh—I even threw away the keys to my pickup— and he'd get them every time.

***

Winters when Gittle Gray owned the Upper Store on the Island, he had a big, pot-bellied stove cranked up in the middle of the room. The health department wasn't in everybody's business in those days and Leroy liked lying by that stove. One night we sat there with Fulton Fisher and two or three other neighbors. Across the road from the store, a big hole had been dug out and ice was laying in the bottom of it.

I told Fulton, I can throw this knife of mine over there across the road in the dark and Leroy here will find it.

Oh hell, he can't do nothin' of the sort, said Fulton, a little guy with set opinions.

We liked to get Fulton going, so we all went out on

Fulton Fisher, a regular at Miss Nora's store.

the porch. Down in the bottom of that hole lay maybe six inches of water, but I thought the skim of ice was hard enough to hold. I sat Leroy and threw my knife. I heard ice break and knew he'd have to find it under water.

Gittle said, That's all of that.

I sent Leroy off and said, He'll be back in a few minutes.

About five minutes later, he came on back and opened his mouth and dropped the knife.

Fulton said, He's the best damn dog in the world.

I didn't argue.

***

Dog pills against heartworms weren't around at that time and Leroy got infested. He started slowing down and coughing. He got so bad I had to lift him into the truck, but he wouldn't stay behind if he saw me getting ready to go hunting. We went up to the gunning club one night, just me and Leroy. He lay in his spot by the stove, bleeding a bit from the mouth.

I said, Come on, ol' fella. You can't go on like this.

I took him out and got my pistol from under the seat of my pickup. I sat him down there in the field and aimed at his head. He cocked his head and looked at me. No way in the world could I shoot that dog. We went back inside and I laid down. Leroy slept that night beside my bed, but didn't last many nights after that.

***

Someone gave me another big, strong Chesapeake after Leroy, but cats scared that dog to death. We had two cats home and that dog would jump through the window to get away from them. A cat must have done something to him when he was a pup.

***

In the '70s I had Charlie, my Black Lab, another good, all-around dog. He liked nutria hunting as much as Leroy had, but didn't try to grab them after getting cut a couple times. From then on, Charlie stayed within a hundred yards of me. He'd follow a nutria's scent and hold it at bay, barking for me to come up and shoot.

Like with Leroy, I could roll an egg across the kitchen floor to Charlie and he'd bring it to me without cracking it. Charlie retrieved the best I ever saw. I've seen him retrieve three ducks at one time—two in his mouth and pushing the third through the water with his nose.

Before anything could happen to Charlie, I bred him to a Chesapeake, thinking I might get Leroy's nose and Charlie's retrieving. I picked out a pup that looked like Leroy, except he had this happy-looking grin on his face all the time. I named the pup Chuck.

Eva "Casey" Thomas, at her usual spot, observing life at Miss Nora's store.

I had a neighbor, Eva Thomas, we called Casey. Casey was a good judge of people, but didn't usually pay much attention to dogs. She studied Chuck, though, and that grin on his face.

Chuck's not serious-minded, she decided. He wants to make a joke out of everything.

Casey was right. Somehow Chuck wasn't cut out for a working dog. One day I took him along with me up the creek. I was moving along at a pretty good clip—Chuck standing up in the bow of the skiff, ears flapping in the wind. I started around a bend, Chuck standing there one second, gone next thing. I heard this thunk, thunk, thunk. He'd fallen overboard and his head was hitting under the skiff. I just did get the engine swung up in time or he'd have gotten hurt, but I got him back aboard okay.

I took him out to get used to me shooting over him, but that wiped his grin off. He was gun-shy and I couldn't break him of it. He made good company, though, tagging along everywhere, as long as I didn't have any firearms.

One December day, Chuck waited outside the door of Nora's store. Sherwood Moore was getting ready to drive the fire engine up to Cambridge to get in the Christmas parade.

Chuck could go with us, Sherwood said. He'd make a good mascot sitting up in there as the fire dog. Only I'm afraid some truck might backfire and we'd never find him again.

***

In his day Sherwood was the best shot on the Island. On day he took his dog, Buster, gunning with him and another guy down the shore here and they shot five or six geese.

Sherwood said, Go get 'em Buster.

Buster didn't move, so Sherwood said, Gawddam it, go get 'em.

The geese were floating away from him, so he pulled his boots up and jumped overboard and waded after them.

Back on shore, boots sloshing full of water, he threw the geese down by the dog and said, Buster old boy, that's how you do it.

Chapter 23

COMMERCIAL FISHING

Dick Shorter used to say I could smell a muskrat or a fish—that it was born right into me. I wish it was that easy. Some years the spring weather turned so crazy I couldn't put enough days of work together to know what the fish were doing. We'd get some twine overboard and it would freeze up, so we couldn't get it back. If the lawmen found it before we did, we lost it, but generally it lay under the ice where they couldn't see it. When we'd finally get a few days to work, we wouldn't see any perch. We'd been frozen out of the river so long, I wouldn't know if perch had come and gone, or maybe hadn't gotten there yet. If we caught a few herring, I'd think to myself, perch comes before herring. The perch must have moved on. I'd go up above the Island and, if I got lucky, I'd hit them and get a couple hundred pounds.

***

My Uncle Dave used to keep a pound net in the Blackwater River, just by Mamma Robbins' house. The way a pound net's set up, a leader steers fish into the pound and it's hard for them to find their way back out. As long as he kept his net in good shape, Uncle Dave could easily go just by the house there and dip out what he wanted. Daddy fished a little bit too, but he didn't really have time for rigging and mending nets. I first fished seriously in the Nanticoke River with a state trooper, Frankie Horsman, who went on his off-days. Then I fished with my brother-in-law, Sammy Robinson.

***

Drift netting is how we fished—rigging weights down

the bottom of a net and corks down the top, so we could lay it out and it would bounce along and go with the tide. The colder it is, the more fish you'll catch. When it gets real cold, they school up. If we guessed right and got to the right place on the right tide, with the right size of mesh, fish struck the net and got gilled. We caught rock, perch, herring, trout, hardhead. We caught bluefish, which are darn mean. A blue bit the tail out of Sammy's oil pants one day.

Once a pound netter figures out where to set up, his rig is stationary. We moved around drift netting, but I fished mostly in the Nanticoke River and

Sammy Robinson

around Fishing Bay. I fished out in Chesapeake Bay for a while with Johnson Robinson, but I didn't like it. I'd be in the stern pulling in our net with waves coming over, lifting me off the deck—sometimes banging me up against the cabin.

Johnson put out three thousand feet of net. In the thickest fog, when we couldn't hardly see each other across the boat, he could go anywhere on Chesapeake Bay he wanted, put that net out, and get it back. His wife had some kind of built-in radar, too. I don't know how she did it. We fished all over the Bay and, wherever we went into harbor, she'd be there in the pickup waiting. If he ever used a telephone, I'd understand, but he never called her. She'd be waiting there just the same, anywhere we docked.

***

I fished closer to home with Sammy Robinson, who was nice to work with. Sammy never got mad or cussed at anything. We fished the Nanticoke one morning near some other guys and had three nets run together and tangle up. It took us forever to untangle them, but Sammy wasn't mad. We finally got straight and got ours back overboard. First thing, one got tangled up on some stumps on the bottom.

I was cussing, but Sammy wasn't saying nothing, so I looked over and asked, Ain't you mad? Don't you feel like cussing?

Sammy said, We all have a certain number of temptations to go through.

I asked him, Do I have to go through all mine in one day?

***

Sammy lived all his life like that, a good Christian gentleman. One morning, when Maryland first had a million dollar lottery prize, me and Sammy were driving along before daylight, trailing the boat to put it over down to Lewis Wharf.

I said, Sammy, I might be sittin' on a million dollars this mornin'.

How's that?

I glanced over to him and said, I got a ticket on the million dollar lottery here in my pocket. Didn't you take a chance?

I'm taking enough chance goin' out with you, he said, never cracking a smile.

***

Me and Sammy were drift-netting the Nanticoke together. In the spring, you could smell when the big fish came up to spawn. It could be blowing fifty miles-an-hour and there would be neither ripple on the water, that's how much spawn they put out in that river. Spawning went on for two or three weeks, different ones coming and going, and it was hard to keep away from catching the big ones. In those days Maryland didn't allow us to keep rockfish over fifteen pounds, which isn't much fish to eat.

One morning, we began pulling fish from our net. We had about thirty oversize rockfish aboard out of the first part of the net when we saw a couple DNR cops coming up fast in a Boston Whaler.

Whatta we gonna do? said Sammy. We can't throw these fish overboard without them seein' us.

I said, If they come close, make like you're pullin' up the net, but just let it slip through your hands. Don't let 'em see we're catchin' any fish.

So that's what we did. Where we'd already pulled the fish out, we slid our hands along without moving the net, trying to look like two guys pulling up empty. The Whaler pulled up close enough for the cops to hail us.

You catchin' anything? one asked.

Not a thing, Officer, I told him, still sliding hand over hand along the net. We're pullin' up, gettin' ready to pack it in.

They went on by, but if they'd listened good they'd have heard my knees knocking.

***

At the time Maryland's DNR prosecuted us for keeping any rock over fifteen pounds. In truth, they should have wanted the big ones caught, so the young rock would have a chance to grow. Around March we started catching the spring run, and in all the years we fished the rock coming to spawn, we never hurt them. There were no regulations to speak of when I started, and rock came back every year thicker than ever. It hurt the spawning stock when they stopped us from fishing the big females that we called cows.

The DNR sent all these biologists to figure out what was going on. It wouldn't have taken me fifteen minutes to teach them what they were trying to learn. A thirty- or forty-year-old cow has done her spawning, but she's eating up everything there is to eat in the river. To have young fish, you have to allow those old cows to be caught.

The biggest rock I ever caught drifting a gill net weighed eighty-one pounds. A fish that size is like a vacuum cleaner scarfing up what's on the bottom—soft crabs, fish, everything. They eat their own and suck up the younger fish's spawn too. When you filet out one of those old cows, you don't need to be no biologist to know what's inside. A good-sized rock might have fifteen or twenty fish inside—some a foot long. That's your future spawning stock getting gobbled up.

I told this marine policeman back in the '80s, You're creating a monster. You'll never have no small fish till some of these big ones start to decline.

He laughed at me then, but he came back years later and said, Wylie, you were right.

I said, Right about what?

He said, You told me we wouldn't have small rock till the big ones declined.

I worked in them every day and I knew. Any year you see plenty of crabs, there aren't many rockfish. Like this year [2004] there's crabs, but you have to go down the bay to catch any fish at all. Besides eating their own young, rock eat up the soft crabs. Then, when the rockfish get too thick, they start getting a disease into them. Nature would balance things out if they'd let her be.

***

We weren't hurting the rock with those nets, but according to Maryland's DNR in the 1980s, we weren't allowed to keep them over fifteen pounds. They'd reversed themselves on the regulation for a while before that, then they put it back in. They switched from pounds to inches, then before long they went to pounds again. One or two seasons, they had fishing cut off down close to Lewis Wharf. A little ways upriver from Vienna, Maryland, the Nanticoke turned into Delaware water, where those same big rock were legal to catch and sell. I tried to keep a Delaware man with me and sell in Delaware, but if I brought them back into Maryland from Delaware, the man could stop me. I was interstating, so I guess I broke the law.

They'd call a public meeting in Annapolis, saying they wanted to discuss next season's regulations. Guys came from all around the Bay, Smith Island on up, packing the hearing room, but we all knew it was just a show. They already had their minds made up what they were gonna do. They sat back laughing to theirselves, and whatever we said at the hearing made no difference.

What we watermen should have done was put up $100 apiece to hire a lobbyist who knew his way around. Having two or three hundred guys at a hearing didn't mean a thing. And in back of the hearing room, there would be DNR cops with their guns, or in plainclothes with walkie-talkies. You'd never think we held licenses bought from the state to run businesses. They treated us like a bunch of desperados.

***

My neighbor Sherwood Moore told me one time, It would fix the DNR if we all refused to buy any licenses or stamps for a year.

I told him, No it wouldn't fix 'em, and I'll tell you why. They'd get on television saying the DNR needs help saving everything. Some stupid sonsabitches would send them all the money they want.

Sherwood said, You're probably right.

I said, I know I am, and they got two of everything now. I saw two of 'em goin' up the river the other day in a boat, towing two Whalers. And there's not a soul on the river but a few trappers going back and forth.

It's a terrible thing to say, but sometimes I think the country would be better off with another depression and all the money dry up. Money is ruining this country.

***

I'd get aggravated like that, then something good would happen. My daughter-in-law Pam's brother Bruce McCready lived up on land, but he kept a little skiff and a hundred-foot net.

Bruce called me up one day, saying he wanted to get a mess of fish to eat.

I said, Come on down and we'll go out and try 'em.

We put this little skiff overboard just above the Island across from Leila Gray's and started running out the net.

Bruce said, Something's breakin' the water.

Putting the last cork over, I said, The corks are all goin' down. Something's goin' on.

We started pulling it up, and I never saw anything like it. Fish were solid in there from one end to the other.

I told Bruce, I've seen 'em solid like that before on one end of a net, but not clear across.

We pulled 435 pounds of perch out of that little net he had. I'll tell you what, it's a pretty sight. It makes it worth all the stuff you got to put up with, just to see something like that.

Chapter 24

TONGING GOOD DAYS AND BAD

In former days, the law said that when we tonged oysters, we had to do everything by hand. When a man got too old to stand up on the washboards and raise the rakes, he went to culling. If we'd had power-winders back when oysters grew thick, tonging would have been easier than going to the office every morning. We would have caught our twenty-five bushel limit in twenty-five minutes. Even doing it all by hand, in the Choptank River I caught thirty bushels in thirty minutes one foggy morning. I tonged 20-foot shafts around middleway of the bridge in Cambridge, about the time the state opened up Robinsons Lump after having it closed for years. That's the thickest I ever saw—oysters as big as your hand and yellow as gold. Once in a while we saw a dead box, but mostly we could tong them right in without culling. The morning they opened it up, I had Willie and Louella with me, each of us allowed twenty-five bushels. We set right there and loaded the boat—caught seventy-eight bushels by 10 o'clock.

Tongers jammed the Choptank as thick as the oysters that day. When it blowed, boats would sheer over on you, so you had to take your foot and push them off. Sammy was there with Omroe Morris. They had their fifty.

When we came in Cambridge Creek with our catch, trucks from all over lined Long Wharf and on down the creek—both sides. Miles Rhodes sailed up there with the *Shamrock*. We sold to some other Crisfielders. I think we got five dollars a bushel from Bozman Brothers. I remember two other brothers from Somerset County buying oysters on the dock that day. Each stood behind his own truck, where his brother couldn't see him, trying to wave us down to stop and sell to him instead of to his brother. They couldn't hack it together and tried to get ahead of each other. Those brothers probably never worked an old double-ender together, having to get along, like me and Jimmy did.

***

When we had oysters around home, I liked selling to Dot and Billy Ruark. For a while, they drove a truck around from Hoopers Island. Early in the season, Dot would get up and pick seventy pounds of crabmeat before driving around to Elliotts Island to buy oysters. She or Billy were always nice to talk to. Most buyers grumble about how much money they lost on the jag you sold them the day before. When you come in from a day of tonging, you don't want to hear that mess.

You want someone like the Ruarks, who tell you, Those are some pretty oysters.

***

Drought caused a lot of damage to oysters in the '80s. Drought affects oysters the same as moving them too far from water they're used to. There's not enough difference in salinity to hurt oysters transplanted from about Crisfield to Annapolis, but if you move them farther, you'll kill them.

Twenty years after the mid-60s die-off, oysters had come back good around home and we were working right along, but up and down cycles happen on the water. This next die-off struck in 1982, the season after Willie graduated and got married.

After a long dry summer, I tried a few oysters outside the Island harbor and they tasted just like Chincoteagues—so salty they nearly drew my mouth up. I knew then we were in trouble. The water wasn't right. When the season opened, me and Willie went out and my brother-in-law, Sammy Robinson, and his boy Timmy were out too. Both our boats found nothing but boxes—empty shells. Between four of us, we took all the first day to catch fifteen bushels.

We decided to go oystering up to Talbot County, then one of the guys down to the Lower Creek—I believe it was Harvey Waller—said, They're all dead up there 'round St. Michaels.

I thought to myself, I know that's not so, 'cause I went up there last week and tried 'em. Me and Willie and Robert had tried up and down that river and pulled up all we wanted. We'd gotten fifteen and twenty and twenty-five oysters a lick—everywhere the same.

Harvey said, I been up there yesterday and tried 'em and they're dying bad—runnin' right out of the shell.

I didn't say nothing, but thought, they ain't gonna die that fast. I had to see it to believe it, so we took a boat up there. The first day, I think we caught twelve bushels among six of us. They were steady dying, just like Harvey said.

Oysters can die fast, real fast. We had to go up to the Chester River to find oysters for a while.

Working away from home waters can get you into trouble. A bunch of us worked out of Oxford one year when there were plenty oysters up there. Me and Willie caught a bunch one morning, then went looking for more. We could go around and see spots of oysters, Willie sitting on the bow of the boat directing me when he saw a dark spot in the water. Jimmy had been on a little spot this same morning and caught about thirty-five bushels real fast. We had about twenty-five for ourselves when me and Willie went looking around some.

We saw another spot and called Jimmy on the radio saying, Jimmy, there's plenty of them over here.

He came on over and so did a few others. About that same time I left to get Robert, who was going to VoTech High

School in Cambridge. I picked him up at the harbor in Oxford afternoons after school to work the rest of the day out. I went ashore down to that lower point going into the creek at Oxford. Me and Willie collected Robert there and went back out.

I said, We'll have a sandwich before we start.

Me and the boys sat there eating, when here come two DNR police Whalers out of the creek from Oxford.

They pulled up and one said, You're tonging polluted bottom.

We asked, Where's the line? What's closed?

This officer pointed from one side of Tred Avon River to the other saying, It's an imaginary line running from that brick house to somewhere around that house over there.

Somewhere could be anywhere, Willie said.

They charged every boat there with harvesting oysters on polluted ground. We didn't know nothing then, but come to find out an old sign marked some closed bottom from half a mile away in the marsh. The officers made every boat around there shovel their catch overboard on that site they said was polluted. Willie and Robert were arguing and wouldn't put ours out.

These oysters weren't caught here, they said, and we're not leaving 'em here.

They were both going to jail before they'd shovel those oysters overboard. I took up our shovel and started putting the catch out, then they helped me do it.

Jimmy and two other boats' captains got tickets and lost their catch. I got charged and lost mine the same way, even though they hadn't seen me do nothing but eat a bologna sandwich.

Poor Jimmy. Since he'd come there and set up, he hadn't caught a gallon of oysters. He had to dump all his bushels he'd caught at his first spot. To make things worse, he had his wife and his mother-in-law and father-in-law working aboard with him. His mother-in-law was putting it on that police captain. I know she said something to me too, for calling Jimmy.

We all chipped in together to hire a lawyer out of Baltimore named Murphy. He sent somebody over to meet us and go looking for any posting saying that bottom was closed. We'd worked different spots around that bank all season and never seen any sign yet. Finally we found a little-bitty sign stuck back in the marsh behind some waterbushes saying that bottom was closed.

Trial day we met Murphy at the Easton courthouse. He went in, looked at the judge, then turned right around and came back to where we waited in the hall.

He told us, We'll set it for another time. That hanging judge is in there. You don't want him.

The marine police were hot about that. They had about fifteen of us hauled in there and thought they were gonna get a mess of convictions that day. The second time we went to the courthouse, the marine police walked in carrying a big freshly-painted signboard banning the harvest of oysters. It was three or four times bigger than the weather-beaten board we'd found in the waterbushes and photographed.

The judge had everybody wait outside so they couldn't hear each other testify. In our case, the officer never saw me or my boys harvesting nothing. There were plenty of witnesses to that.

When I came out, one of the officers came over to me.

How'd you make out, Wylie?

Good, I said. He found us not guilty.

He can't do that, he said.

I said, Well, the judge just done it.

In the end, everybody got clear. The judge could see that sign had never spent a night out in the marsh. Still, we had the lawyer to pay, plus we all lost two days' work for court dates, and our catch from that first day.

If I'm caught fair and square, I'll not say much about paying my fine, but I don't want to be railroaded by some officer bending the law, or charged under some fool regulation that makes no sense.

***

Late in the '80s, oysters south of Talbot County died. I trailed the T-Craft up to Oxford and me and Robert and Willie progged around the Tred Avon. One spot was so deep, our tongs wouldn't reach bottom unless we worked with our hands underwater, but we felt a pocket of oysters down there. You can only work your hands in the river for so long in November. Power-winders had gotten legal then, as long as you didn't raise the heads above water with them, so we went to the Messick brothers in Bivalve and got a pair of 28s made up—paid ten dollars a foot.

Next day out of Oxford, both boys wanted to try but couldn't do nothing with them, the motion is so different. You have to spread the heads, then rake slowly. Then you hold them together a couple beats for the heads to close. There's so much flex and such a distance for the motion to travel up and down to register.

I stood on the washboards working the tongs and the pedal for the winders. The shafts stay pretty stable as long as the heads are underwater, but they start taking off as soon as the heads break the surface. One of the boys had to grab the head by hand and help guide it into the boat and over the cull board. You can't work 28s at all if it's blowing or the tide running. The tide twists the heads around on the shafts.

The first day we worked those 28s, we caught twenty-four bushels of the biggest kind of oysters. Other boats were all around us, but nobody else had tongs to reach that hole.

***

We haven't had any oysters around home for years, till they showed back up in Tangier Sound this year, 2004. Those oysters should be up here, because Fishing Bay's fresher water than Tangier Sound. When they die off, oysters in saltier water go first. That's why we could travel up the Potomac or north up the Choptank or Tred Avon or Chester River and get a day's work when nothing grew to legal size around home.

I believe the oysters are living south of here in saltier water because they don't get all the spray and experimenting the state and other agencies do in the marsh around Fishing Bay. Instead of spraying mosquitoes on the Island where the people are, they aerial spray thousands of acres of marsh. All these creeks and rivers feeding into Fishing Bay pick up every chemical from all the spraying they do against mosquitoes and phragmites and roadside weeds and who knows what else. Where they're catching oysters this year is farther from that kind of spraying.

They spray around our marsh for phragmites, testing to see what they can do. They ain't gonna kill phragmites. They sprayed once and killed some growing twenty feet in the air, but the phragmites came right back.

The county roads people are death on weeds growing along bridges over the waterways, but don't like to get out of their trucks. A county man went along spraying from inside the truck below Savannah Lake one day and I stopped and asked what they used. The man named off something or other.

I asked him, Is it anything like weed-killer you get in the hardware store?

Something on that order, he said.

Overnight everything turned brown everywhere they sprayed, by Pokata and Island Creeks, and along all the little bridges. That's potent stuff. I had a couple bottles of week-killer at home, but after I saw what it did, I left mine sitting right in the garage.

Chapter 25

TONGING AND CRAB-POTTING THE WESTERN SHORE

There's a different law working over on the Potomac River. Virginia owns one shore and Maryland the other. The river itself is Maryland's, but either state's cops can come and write you up for something. When oysters grew real thick over there, we got boarded twice a day, once by each state. Virginia was harder on us than Maryland. When you saw the Virginia man coming, you could consider yourself getting a ticket for something.

We were just working along one day when Newton Ruark all of a sudden dropped his culling hammer and started pulling up the killick, an iron weight to hold us over oyster rock.

We gotta do somethin', he said. That man's comin' right down here on us.

He already had the killick back aboard, so I hopped down off the washboard, seeing it was a Virginia boat, and cranked her up. We circled around and the man went right on by us. If he'd come aboard, he'd have overhauled everything and wrote us up for something—small oysters or wrong equipment or something. The Maryland man generally gave us a break at that time on the Potomac, but not Virginia.

Virginia being stricter on watermen was the opposite of what went on over there a few years before my time. War broke out around Cobb Island, Maryland and Colonial Beach, Virginia a few years before Daddy first went there with me and Jimmy. Maryland's marine police ran out of control, chasing watermen and shooting up boats and towns. It's a wonder they killed just one guy, but they wounded others, including shooting each other accidentally—friendly fire. This shooting war in the late 1950s broke out over nothing but oysters. I tonged then, but caught enough oysters in Fishing Bay to keep me working close to home, thank goodness.

***

I've never been shot at by the police on the Potomac, but I've been harassed otherwise. The worst one was a Maryland cop, Natural Resource Police they were called in the '80s, when I sailed over in Willie's Sea Hawk with him and Robert. This officer was so bad, we come to find out, nobody on Cobb Island would even sell him gas. They had three places to gas up and he had to stay in the patrol boat at all three. They wouldn't let him on the bank at the marinas.

The locals called him Rick the Prick. The same day he first came aboard us, he'd gone up to a truck driver taking in oysters asking, You got your buyer's license?

The boy said, Yeah.

Give it here, he said.

When he couldn't find nothing wrong with the license, instead of handing it back to the boy, he wadded it up and threw it on the parking lot.

I didn't know nothing about no Rick the Prick. The first time he boarded us, the oysters looked pretty good. We're allowed a few mistakes, five percent. He culled them out, measuring them with his gauge, and charged us with too many undersized oysters. Okay, it cost us a fine, but I thought no more about it that day. Next day, he boarded us again. Five percent of a bushel isn't many oysters, but we'd been extra careful that second day, measuring every close call. The second trip he had a female officer with him. She was okay, but he jumped aboard and started shoving the culling board and throwing the tongs down, bending the head and chipping the gel coat on the side of the boat. Both officers had brass measuring gauges. Oysters took up on her gauge, measuring over three inches, but they went right through his. He was throwing nice oysters out again.

I said, What are you throwin' out there?

Undersize oyster, he said.

These ain't no undersize oysters. They been measured every one.

Watch this, he said, passing one right on through his gauge and setting it aside on the culling board.

Robert got hot and he told Robert, Get up on that cabin and shut up or I'm taking you to jail.

Look here, Willie said, hitting oysters on the gauge he'd borrowed from the girl.

Rick said, My gauge is the only one that counts in this river. These oysters are undersized and I'm sending them to kingdom come.

With that, he shoved that pile overboard, one more wrong thing he done that day. In the first place, if they were undersized, they should go back where they got taken up. He'd stopped us when we were running into the harbor, then shoved the oysters overboard on polluted bottom

That's when I came to my senses. Sometimes the man handles an oyster rough checking it, so the thinner new growth on its lip breaks off and it won't measure up to three inches. This guy did something different, though. He'd done something to his gauge. The other officer hadn't, so measuring the same pile, they got different answers. He made her write the ticket, though, charging us with nine percent of our catch being undersized.

I said, Man, that's fines two days in a row. We're gonna carry this to court.

He said, Do what you want, but this is *my* river.

Willie asked him, What's your problem? We treat your guys right when they come over our way.

He didn't think we'd go to court, being from the Eastern Shore. He'd done some Hoopers Islanders the same way. Early their first day over there, they only had two bushels when he came aboard. They got so disgusted they turned around and sailed home. We left, too, after that second day, but we got Sam Kenney to represent us and went back next spring to LaPlata for a day in court. We lost money taking off from fishing to go around there, but we figured that officer had filed his gauge down. That's why a legal-sized oyster would pass through without touching.

Sam had all the witnesses sequestered. We waited out in the hallway while each other testified. Lawyers for the next cases were jammed up out there for three or four hours while our case dragged on.

They were saying, What's going on in there?

Willie told the judge, The officer boarded us like a storm trooper or a wild man, damaging my boat and equipment.

The judge seemed pretty unhappy about our case costing his morning.

Before letting us off, he asked Rick, Officer, are you a storm trooper?

No, Sir. I'm not.

Then you must be a wild man, the judge said. I don't think these boys would come all the way from Elliotts Island—wherever the hell that's at—if they didn't think they were right.

***

The first place I ever crab-potted was over on there to Calvert County. Jimmy was crab-potting around Cove Point the first part of August one year. I worked at Dupont then. Jimmy was about ready to quit going potting, then I got laid off.

He said, Come on go crab-potting with me.

I said, All right.

We met at Hoopers Island and went over in his boat. We set out a hundred and thirty crab-pots and caught about two thousand pounds of sooks and thirty or forty baskets of jimmys one day. Over where we caught them, water was so clear you could see the crabs in pots in five or six feet of water. Jimmy and some of those boys over there wanted to go up in the Patuxent to some beer joint, but I wanted to get back home. We had to cross the Bay in that little 32-foot boat Al Garcia sold him, *Miss Candy*, with all those crabs aboard— too many crabs for that boat. We sold to Russell Hall at Hoopers Island, then I had to drive all the way around to Elliotts Island. We worked over there five or six weeks.

There's a terrorist watch now where we worked. I saw those docks by our old fishing ground on television. They won't let anybody crab now by the nuclear power plant at Calvert Cliffs, where we caught that load. That was the only crab-potting I ever did till I went to Texas in '77.

***

Closer to home, another place I used to go crab-potting was down seaside around Public Landing, below Snow Hill. One year before parasailing and water skiing started, me and Ray Moore went behind Ocean City to Assawoman Bay, around 125th Street, and set pots out, but we didn't catch much. Below there in Sinepuxent Bay, there's a lot of crabs. Me and Ray went there for hard crabs early in the spring, then after that we shedded out softcrabs. A guy there had eighty floats we kept going for him around the clock. As soon as we finished fishing them, it was time to start again. The main thing was to get the crabs out of the water in the floats quick when they came out of their shell. Otherwise, they start hardening up.

We went in the floats with both hands and scooped them out and packed them—so many in a box, sorted by size and straightened up the way they should go. Then the guy who had the place carried them to Crisfield.

We could see the crabbers peeler-potting right out in front of the place. Those boys down there brought peelers in by the thousands. We shedded out 702 dozens one night. That run only lasts about eight days, then dwindles right on down. We made money in that week though. He paid us $1.50 a dozen.

The last time I went down there, that guy had sold to a new man from the city. The new owner didn't want to work hard. He didn't know nothing about crabs neither, but he wouldn't leave us alone. He was all the time on us about something.

I said, Ray, we ain't got to do this. What do we want to do this for?

After that, I set up my own floats on the Island down to the Lower Creek. The county got on me about that, though, so I talked to Delema Jones and moved my floats to her place by the Upper Creek.

Chapter 26

NUTRIA

Nutria are pretty much giant rats, by which I don't mean muskrats. Nutria are South American rodents somebody imported into the States. They're a lot meaner than a muskrat, which is scared of you. I've never been charged by a muskrat, but I've had a couple close calls when nutria came at me.

The first nutria in Dorchester County were carried up from Louisiana during the Depression. Fur dealers and the government brought a few pairs up here and breeding got out of hand, till nutria became a real nuisance, crowding out muskrat and tearing up marsh. A nutria is stronger than a muskrat, bigger and slower, with two sets of great long, wide, brown teeth sticking out, the bottom set longer than the top. They started spreading from around Blackwater Refuge, tearing up grasses by the roots and turning marsh into mud flats. Now my youngest son Cory's working on a government program to get rid of them, but when we had a good market for fur, we knocked them back ourselves. They make a pretty coat.

For years my father trapped the big piece of marsh above Shorters Wharf Bridge called Jobes Point. Now the government's running that too. Back in the 1950s, when I started working with Daddy, there weren't many nutria around there. Daddy's marsh joined up with Blackwater marsh. He had a ditch dug all the way around his. That ditch got thicker and thicker with nutria every year, till Daddy was fighting a real war against them. He had so many, Daddy said a nutria would walk around looking for a trap to get into. But being bigger than muskrat, they just messed up traps set for 'rats, and if one bled around a trap, that attracted more.

A muskrat builds his house, then he wants quiet. Nutria don't build houses, they just put down sedge and lie on top of it. They'll come along and dig up the straw on top of a muskrat's house after he's done all the work. Them fooling around on top bothers the muskrat, especially in the mating season.

***

A dog that liked hunting nutria helped in a big way. A good dog would go in brush and push the nutria out. He might get cut once in a while, but anytime you wanted to go after

nutria, he'd be ready. Right in the heat of his nutria war, Daddy had a Black Lab he took out with him. He fitted a kind of helmet for the dog's head and a piece of stovepipe for his throat. He tried making dog vests out of sailcloth and leather, but the nutria would

Nutria

rip them off or bite right through. Any little nick that dog got, Daddy ran him to the vet. He was running him to Cambridge near about every day. One time his dog chased five nutria into a pond and they stopped and waited for that dog. They all piled on him and liked to drown him, but somehow the dog got away.

Daddy tickled me to death. He was in a battle, loaded with nutria every ten feet, trying to keep them down, and he wasn't doing nothing. They increased more every year. Like most of the older men, Daddy carried a walking stick to lean on a little bit, or to help himself pull up out of a pot hole if he mis-stepped. It could come in handy, too, if a nutria jumped at him. Daddy was usually a sure thing with a stick.

Out in the marsh with him once during a hard freeze,

I had my Chesapeake, Leroy, along. Daddy had his walking stick and he struck at a nutria that day and hit my dog instead. Leroy was okay. Man, though, Daddy was tore up.

I said, That's all right, Dad. You didn't mean to do that.

But he wouldn't strike at another nutria the rest of the day. Another day, Leroy was on a nutria that led him into a pond. He got within about a foot of the nutria and it turned around and went for him. I was a ways off when I saw what that nutria was gonna do and shot it. It scared me after I did it, I was so close to hitting that dog, but in a pond a dog hardly stands a chance against a nutria..

By the 1970s nutria spread all around Fishing Bay and beyond. We had no market for them, neither fur nor meat. To keep them down some, we used to shoot them and leave them lay, just to ease pressure off the muskrats and marshes. Going up Island Creek you could kill a hundred nutria on one trip. Then in 1977 a man named Forrest Bond came in here, a fur buyer from Indiana, offering five dollars apiece for nutria. That's the first time we ever had a market for them. Later that same season, everything froze up tight and stayed that way from January till the end of February.

Muskrat runs froze up and muskrats hunkered down in their beds and stayed there. You can't set no traps with heavy ice like that. Muskrats ain't moving noways; they're laying back on top of each other. Nutrias weren't used to that much cold. To keep warm, they huddled on top of muskrat houses. We'd find seven or eight piled up there froze to death, the house stove in and muskrats smothered inside.

Nobody could work marsh they'd rented for muskrating, but we had that market with Mr. Bond and caught a load of nutria. We got five dollars apiece from him, and didn't have to skin them unless we wanted to. We got five dollars in the round, and no more if we skinned them. We took as high as two pickup loads a day. Our problem was getting them all out of the marsh. If we'd had an all-terrain vehicle like an Argo to help run them out to the road, there's no telling how many we could have taken.

Me and Grant and Sammy worked together. Sometimes Jimmy came hunting with us and Dougie Eberspacher, Donnie Bowman, a couple Windsors from over river. Sammy's boys and mine came when they weren't in school. Some of us had dogs we took along too.

Selling nutria in the round was easiest, but a man could only carry so many across the marsh, four or five whole nutria—six at the most. Besides being too heavy to tote, nutria skinned a lot easier before they stiffened up in the cold. We'd find an old duck blind to get in out of the wind. A couple of the better skinners worked in there while the others hunted.

It was punishment. We built a fire in a corner of a blind, but it was still cold. Neither flake of snow fell, though, to make it hard walking. We hunted over a thousand acres of marsh and, but for the cold, could have walked it in tennis shoes. We usually met around Savannah Lake, parked on the turn there, and walked five miles along the edge of the woods to Island Pond. A couple big duck blinds stood around that pond. We started there and worked our way back towards the road.

***

We'd given Robert a 3-wheeled all-terrain vehicle for Christmas that winter. I started taking that, and Donnie Bowman had a dune buggy we used too. We loaded on as many hides as they could hold. The nutria we left in the round, we knotted onto a string, to make them easier to handle. I had them hanging on the handlebars and trailing behind, dragging out to the road.

After we got them from the marsh, we still had a job finding a place to put them all. After school, I had my garage filled with boys skinning, Martinek boys and my boys and Sammy's. Over in Robbins, Allen Smith and Jimmy Robbins had fur houses buying for Mr. Bond and everybody in Robbins was skinning nutria too.

***

Temperatures dropped down below zero The radio kept warning, don't go out unless it's an emergency, but we went all over. We hunted state marsh from Guinea to Elliotts Island. Guinea Island, where me and Jimmy did field work as kids, lies across Island Creek from Savannah Lake, five miles off from the road. With everything froze up, you could go anywhere you wanted. Trapping muskrat, if you didn't own marsh, you rented the right to trap it, but there was no law on nutria, and we hunted public marsh.

I had a couple dogs I took with me, my Black Lab Charlie and a smaller Lab named Beazley. A dog can't do much with a muskrat, because that old 'rat knows how to get under the ground. He's fast and he's gonna find a hole to go down. But a nutria will stay right up on the grass and a dog can smell him a mile away. Those dogs of mine loved hunting nutria and learned quick. Old Leroy, my Chesapeake I'd had back in the '60s, knew how to grab a nutria from the back, but all a dog really needs to do is bark. A nutria will back into the bushes looking for a place to hide. Then the dog holds him for me to come up. I carried a .22 rifle and aimed for a head shot. Like most dogs, Charlie and Beazley would run a nutria, but not charge into it. They learned that if they didn't grab a nutria just right, they got cut. Of course, his ears is a vulnerable part of a dog. When I first took him, I had to pack Charlie's ears in snow once or twice, 'cause he'd bleed out from a nicked ear.

A muskrat's scared of a dog. If he's cornered, a 'rat will give a dog that cat-paw or maybe snap at him, but he looks for a hole if he can. A nutria's different. Back in those days it wasn't anything to see eight or ten nutria at a time. If half that many together chased a dog, they could kill him, so you needed to stay close. Fuzzy stood in a class by himself. My brother-in-law had Fuzzy, a big, big Black Lab-St. Bernard mix. Fuzzy loved the cold and hated nutria. He knew just how to grab them. He'd get them from the back and pin them against the ground. Fuzzy'd go a mile ahead of you, kill a nutria, and before you could get there, he'd gone and killed another one. We lost a lot of those that Fuzzy caught.

When a dog's in most danger from a nutria is in water. If a pond's not frozen, a nutria will jump in and swim about middle-way across, then turn around on a dog. Donnie Bowman had a Chesapeake—a grown dog, but not real big. One day that Chesapeake trailed a nutria along a little branch of Island Creek about ten feet wide. The dog followed the shore around, then stopped. He was barking from the bank, and that darned nutria doubled back and reached up, grabbed the dog by the head, and pulled him off the bank right under some ice. Donnie was scared to death he was gonna lose his dog.

I heard him holler, Wylie, he's got my dog!

I ran there. About that time, the dog broke loose and the nutria swam on away under the ice. A Chesapeake's got a heavy coat and the dog never got nicked, but Donnie could've lost him.

One time me and my dog Charlie were chasing a nutria across a frozen pond when it stopped short and turned on us. Charlie went tumbling over the nutria. I tried to put on my brakes, and my feet flew up from under me. My ass hit the ice and I slid feet first straight for that thing. I was kicking, trying to dig my heels into the ice to stop myself. I slid within inches of that nutria—near enough to hear his teeth clicking. They sounded like somebody fast tap, tap, tapping a couple empty cans together. Charlie came up behind the nutria barking and it turned towards Charlie, giving me a chance to scramble to my feet and get an angle to shoot.

Another time I had a nutria near about on my heels and I'd run out of bullets. I took my gun barrel and hit him across the nose and killed him. You don't have to hit him too hard if you know where to pop him.

***

I had marsh rented for muskrating that year across the Nanticoke River and couldn't trap it for the ice. I knew some nutria were on it, so me and Sammy went across the river in a skiff. The ice was eight inches or more deep. We took a couple poles and drove nails in the end of them so they wouldn't slip. We poled right across till we got to the channel. Tugs had come up there, but the channel made ice again, so we got out and pulled the skiff up over the edge where the big cakes of broken ice were piled up. We got the bow up on that pile and pulled the skiff on over and went on about our business. When we got to my marsh on the Wicomico County side, all

Ice breaking against Fishing Point in the 1970s

the nutria were dead—four and five and six on a muskrat bed.

If we'd broken through ice, in the channel or anywhere else, that skiff wouldn't have been no good to us. When I sit back and think about things I done, it makes me shiver right today.

Chapter 27

ANIMAL RIGHTS AND WRONGS

Nutria was one thing my mother never fixed at home. I ate my first nutria one day in Lev Davenport's shanty. Lev had a little shanty right to the mouth of Island Pond that he rented to deer and duck hunters. Some of the stars from Hee Haw used to come there. The shanty burned later in a marsh fire, but still stood in the winter of 1976-77. About 11 o'clock one morning, five or six of us hunting nutria had already eat all our dinners up and were still empty. If you're hungry enough, you'll eat anything, so we went in that shanty and I boiled some nutria. I cut the hind quarters off and boiled a potful down in water. I didn't have a big enough pot or we could have eaten more than what we did. With anything to spice them up, they would have been right nice.

***

Finally, late in that winter, DNR cops caught up with a bunch of us: Sammy and his boys, me and Willie and Robert, the Windsors, Grant Barnett. We were coming back from Island Pond carrying at least eighty skinned hides among us, plus we each had five in the round, all we could handle. About two and a half miles from the road, we seen two men up ahead on one of those little islands out there.

Sammy said, Who do you suppose that is out here . . .nobody nutria hunting.

We got up closer and saw two DNR cops waiting for us to come out. We went on up to where they stood.

One said, We been after you for two days, and all we found was motorcycle tracks everywhere. About 10 o'clock this morning, we finally got one of your men.

We'd sent Donnie out with a buggy-load early that morning and he never came back. We thought he'd broke down.

I told the cops, We thought it was funny Donnie never showed back up. What's the trouble?

He said, You boys are trespassing.

I asked him, How can we be trespassing when we're on public marsh?

He didn't have a good answer, but they made us drop the hides and nutria anyway. They were gonna have us drop them all here and there in separate piles.

I said, We'll drop every one here, all in the same pile.

That's what we all did. It was close to sundown and enough of a moon showed that I took a mark off that on where we were. I was gonna come back.

The man said, We're coming back in the morning on an Argo and pick those furs up.

I said, Help yourself.

We walked on out with them. When we got to the road, they took all our rifles.

After they drove off with them I said, Grant, let's make a run. We can carry them skinned hides. We've got close to a hundred of them and that'll be enough to pay our fines.

It was at least five hundred dollars worth of fur, so me and Grant set back out in the moonlight, the temperature about five below zero. I knew where we'd dropped them, because I took that mark from where we stood to the moon, and to the woods. When those cross up right together, you can reach down and pick up what you dropped, same as aiming a rifle bullet. When we got back out to where our things lay, we left the whole nutrias and loaded up with the hides, better than forty on each of us.

Walking back out, Grant said, I know a shortcut.

I said, Okay, go ahead; we'll use your shortcut.

I followed along after him down this creek, each of us carrying a hundred pounds or more of frozen hides. I heard a little crackling sound once, then a second one. When the third crackling started, I jumped up on the bank.

Grant Barnett by a muskrat house on Guinea Island in 1974.

I heard Grant mumble, Aw Shit!

Down he went in water half-way up his chest, nutria hides on top of him.

Here, I said, hand me them hides.

When I got him up on the bank, Grant cussed me. Damn sumbitch you, you'd let me drown over a nutria. You don't care what happens to me, do you, just them hides?

I said, We don't want to lose them nutria. We worked too hard to be letting them go.

By the time we got to the road, his clothes were all frozen stiff.

That happened on a Saturday and I had a lawyer in Salisbury I talked to and got an appointment for me and Grant Monday morning. We drove down there with the DNR's regulation book to show him.

He asked us, They took your guns? What kind of ticket did they give you?

I said, They never gave us neither ticket.

He said, Then they didn't know what to charge you with. You'll have your guns back in the morning.

***

Back on Saturday, Donnie had left out of the marsh taking a load of unskinned nutria. He crossed to the road on the dune buggy, loaded them into his pickup, and left for my garage on the Island. The DNR cops didn't see him earlier, but were there when he came back to Savannah for another run.

They came over to him asking, What do you think you're doing?

He said, Hauling nutrias.

Tuesday morning, the day after seeing the lawyer, me, Grant, Sammy, and Wayne Windsor were in my garage skinning those nutria Donnie'd hauled out on Saturday. The same DNR cops pulled in the yard.

I said, Boys here they are. The lawyer was right. He said our guns would be back here to the door in the morning.

They opened the garage door and I said, Come on in.

Here they came in the door with arm loads of our rifles.

Technicality in the law, this one said, you're off on a technicality this time.

I think he was really worried we might sue for that fur he thought we'd lost. They never went back out there after those hides, so they didn't know we had them. I knew they'd leave them out there to rot.

***

Louella happened to be in the garage at the time they came. Everything was all right till one cop said something about how, the way things were going, Willie and Robert were gonna end up in jail. When he said that, Louella gave him a tongue-lashing. She had him backed into a corner wagging her finger in his face.

His partner told me later, I hope I never have to face up to any woman like Louella was that day. My partner should've known better than to say something like that about her boys.

***

After the DNR stopped us from working, we started playing. Me and Grant went out doing tailspins in our trucks on Savannah Lake one day. Daniel Martinek was down home on the Island making an ice boat, and when he got up there with it next day, the ice wouldn't hold it. February ice can leave overnight.

***

The regulation book never had the nutria's name in it up to that year, but it was in there the next. It had been a rodent that could be hunted, but they rewrote the book classing it with regulated fur-bearers to stop us from hunting that state land. After that, everything started going to the devil with nutria.

Forrest Bond never had cut his price that year, but he never came back again neither. Nutria kept on multiplying, doing more and more damage. The state talked about paying a bounty to get us hunting them again, but they never did nothing for us. They cooked up recipes trying to make a market for nutria meats, using a ten dollar surcharge tacked on watermen's licenses for seafood marketing campaigns. People didn't bite. As things got worse, they came up with a plan to credit $1.50 per nutria tail against rent due. A trapper renting state marsh for the season could pay his rent in tails, but once he turned in enough to pay the rent, he didn't get nothing more. If we trapped private property, we got nothing at all from the state. It didn't do no good to knock them back on

– 167 –

one parcel of marsh and not the next—as if nutria would know where state property lines ran.

***

The biggest year we trappers ever had down here muskrating, brown 'rats brought eight dollars apiece and black 'rats ten. I believe that was 1983. Then time came there was hardly any market for any kind of fur. Before that time, a woman would buy a beautiful nutria or muskrat coat and feel proud to wear it. Then American women started getting harassed for wearing fur, and the same in Germany and all around Europe, where a lot of our furs sold. Television news went on about animal rights and the fur, the fur. People got scared to wear fur.

***

A few years after wanting to fine us for hunting nutria, after we lost our market for any kind of furs, the state hired some Englishman and paid him to come over here to show them how to kill nutria. This guy had them buy some specially-trained English dog. I don't think that Englishman killed neither nutria before skidding out of here—didn't like the marsh, I guess I don't know what happened to the dog. Maybe the nutria ate him.

Now the government's got a plan to get rid of all the nutria and my son Cory's working on it. I give Cory some advice from time to time, but I think it goes in one ear and out the other. For starts, the government's got the wrong kind of traps. They use a #1 trap and they should have a #2. A bigger trap would make a lot of difference. I'd like to see what that government program could do starting out from scratch, with as many nutria as we faced in '77.

Chapter 28

SALISBURY

I had a good business down to Salisbury in the mid-1970s. During warm weather I retailed seafood out of an old gas station I rented on Route 13.

My friend Teddy Creighton had gone from Dorchester over to Waldorf when slots were big. He had a place on 301 called Frontiertown. When I oystered over there, I couldn't pay for a drink. After the state outlawed slots, he got into crabs, but it wasn't the same.

One day he said, You want some equipment? I'm gonna sell my steamin' rig.

I wasn't really looking for anything. I had my hands full in crabbing season buying and hauling to the city. I went down the cellar with him to look, though, and he offered me a deal on some first-class equipment. He only wanted $800 for the whole rig. I thought I might need it somewhere down the line, so I bought and hauled it home—enough gear to supply crab feasts. I set it up in the garage to see what it would do. It had an oil-powered boiler to make live steam and a line with values to different sizes of pots. I could steam up to a dozen bushels at a time. It started me thinking about cutting out the retailer as well as the middleman.

I looked around and found an old service station in Salisbury. The oil company still owned it, but it had been rented out for a pool hall. When I got the building, I had to clean and paint it up. I did some plumbing, added sinks, then put my equipment in there. I didn't need to buy much more, just a showcase and scales, and I had a pot made up in Seaford to steam five pounds of shrimp at a time. Then I was ready for business. A realtor handled the year's lease and collected the rent, $250 a month.

The realtor said, It sure is nice to have you here. It got rough when this was a pool hall. We had the cops called all the time. Some of the kids who hung around were always starting trouble.

The cops were glad to have me there too, and kept a good eye on the place when I wasn't around. If they saw anything strange going on, they overhauled whoever didn't belong there.

I carried mostly fresh, local seafood. The Wicomico River was close by, so I sold bait too—peelers, bloodworms, nightcrawlers. People caught all kinds of fish on my bait. They were happy to catch a little string of fish to carry home.

Louella worked with me and in January and February we closed and I went trapping and worked with my gunners. In March I re-opened, getting a few crabs out of Virginia and fresh fish. Then the local crabs came on and kept me busy till fall, when oysters came in.

***

People like salty oysters on the half shell. I went down to Chincoteague, Virginia and bought oysters. At least the dealer said they were Chincoteagues. The shells looked like Chincoteagues, which are fat, but don't have a very pretty shape. They have what's called goose-tongue shells, not as round a cup as ours.

One guy bought oysters down home on the Island and carried pickup loads from Fishing Bay to Chincoteague. He sold to a dealer, the uncle of a buddy of mine. The uncle dumped Fishing Bay oysters into floats—wooden troughs he dragged into the water and left overboard for a night to pick up a saltier taste.

One day he told me, They clicked on me overnight.

I said, Whadda you mean?

He said, If you leave them too long, they click.

He meant oysters died if left over-long in water too brine and too different from what they grew in. When they died, the shell opened up, making a little clicking sound.

***

I learned how to make Chincoteagues without driving that far. When I closed my shop in the evening, I took bags of oysters down towards Ocean City and put them overboard for about twenty-four hours, long enough to get them good and salty. It's probably all built up around there now, but I could take Route 50 and go off on Route 90, then take an off-ramp to a dirt lane leading to Assawoman Bay. This little lane ran about one hundred feet before the bay. Nobody bothered you in those days. I could only see a couple house lights off to the left, back in some woods. I parked at the end of this lane to put on my hip boots, then waded three or four burlap bags of oysters out into the water. Next evening I waded out and brought them ashore.

When someone came in for Chincoteagues, I shucked one or two of my Ocean City oysters and said, Here. Try this.

They'd say, Boy that's good. Give me a bushel of them Chincoteagues.

I had five bushels one day and sold them as quick as I could handle them. Finally, I started making my own without going anywhere. I mixed table salt in tap water, tasting till the brine seemed just right. I had a big tub on wheels that would hold about four bushels. People didn't worry about what the shell looked like as long as the oysters tasted salty. A guy stopped there one day.

You carry those salty oysters? he asked.

Yeah.

Are they really salty?

Yeah.

You sure of it?

Come on back here, I said, I'll show 'em to you.

I took him in the back where I made them up and I shucked one and gave it to him. He swished it all around in his mouth and gulped it down.

Damn that's good, he said. Can I get two bushels of 'em?

Before long, I had all the service clubs and fire companies and men's clubs sewed up, supplying their oyster roasts and crab feasts.

***

From its filling station days, a big door opened into the back of the shop. I could back my truck in there to unload. I had my freezer back there where I kept shrimp.

You had to watch people though. I was busy up front one afternoon with some foreign-speaking man from off the highway asking about two dozen jumbo crabs. Louella was there too. Something told me I'd better check in the back. I went back and caught his two boys taking shrimp. They looked to be only about ten and twelve years old. My big door stood ajar just enough for them to slither under to get to my freezer. They had two five-pound boxes of shrimp.

I hollered, What are you boys doing there!

Nothing. Nothing, they said, dropping my shrimp and skittering back out under the door, running to their car.

I picked up the boxes and put them in the freezer and went back to the man and said, Them boys stole my damn shrimp.

He lost what English he had when he came in, mumbling on a bunch of stuff I couldn't understand. He had asked about a couple dozen jumbo crabs, so I put two dozen sooks in a bag and closed it up and charged him top price for jumbos. That's the last I saw of them.

***

Another guy stopped in there asking, Please Mister, I need twenty dollars. My wife's gotten herself collared and I need twenty dollars to bail her out.

I said, Man, I ain't got twenty dollars to bail out your wife.

He said, Please, Mister, I'll even give you the title to my car.

I said to myself, Well, it could be true. Twenty dollars ain't that much.

I give it to him and I never saw him again either. I believe I've still got the title home. He probably had a whole glove compartment full of them.

***

Before long, I had the whole town's seafood business locked up. I sold as high as seventy-six baskets of big crabs in one day. A basket of number ones ran between $20 and $25 at that time. The realtor I dealt with wasn't a customer. He owned a weekend home on the seaside, where he kept a couple crab-pots and caught his own. Fridays he came by and I gave him fish heads for his pots. He hung around watching, smiling, and eyeing everything.

He'd say, You doing a pretty good business here today, aren't you boy?

Yeah, I'm getting rid of a few.

The second year, he doubled the rent up to $500, big money in 1976, but I could cover it. One Fourth of July, I took in over $4,000.

Spring 1977, Louella took a call from the realtor and told me, The realtor called from Salisbury and the rent's going up another $500 a month this season.

I said, Tell him I'll be there Saturday and get that equipment out of there.

I was down in Texas and had to fly home and drive to the shop. I had the equipment halfway torn out when the oil company man who owned the place came by.

What's going on? he asked.

I said, Well, I'm gonna have to leave. Your realtor said you're doubling the rent again.

He said, What did he rent it to you for?

I said, I paid $500 last year and he said you're doubling it again.

The owner said, I raised the rent, but nothing like that.

I should have stayed there, but I was making plenty of money in Texas at the time. The shop took in enough money to cover the increase, but I got disgusted. I didn't like that realtor's actions and I didn't know where his stopping point was going to be. I came to regret getting hot over that, though.

Chapter 29

TRYING TEXAS

The winter of 1976-77 went from a disaster to a bonanza for waterman. Early on, the whole Chesapeake Bay froze up so tight nobody could oyster. We didn't know what in the world we were gonna do. Freeze-ups happen from time to time, but that winter, for the first and last time, a governor of Maryland made watermen eligible for unemployment benefits. I went up to Cambridge to sign up. I didn't know what to do with the paperwork, but this gal filling out her forms at the counter next to me saw me fumbling around.

Don't you know how to fill these out? she asked.

I said, No, I never did.

She set hers aside and said, Give 'em here; I'll help you. I'm eighteen and been drawing for three years.

She knew how to do it all right. Next thing I knew, checks started rolling in. I was getting $80 every two weeks in unemployment and $200 a month food stamps. I thought to myself, Okay, one time in my life I'm gonna see how it feels to live off the government. Some guys got heating oil, too, but I didn't get oil.

Then Forrest Bond came along and bought fur. When we stopped nutria hunting, I heard from a guy who'd gone down south when the bay froze.

He said, I'm catching a-plenty crabs down here in Texas—flying 'em up to Baltimore. Why don't you come down and crab for me?

***

I should have been happy just to kick back and scud

along collecting checks till summer, but I guess Dick Shorter was right about me. Four or five of us were sitting around Nora's store one day. I was between seasons and rambling on about starting a sightseeing business.

I told them, I'm gonna carry bird-watchers up Island Creek in my skiff. I'll charge a hundred dollars a head to show them all the birds up the creek. They'll be happy to pay when they see what I see every day.

Dick Shorter said, You might charge a thousand dollars a trip, but as soon as you heard somebody caught a couple bushels, you'd forget all about birds and go crabbin'.

So in '77, though I'm drawing this money from the government, I said to Grant Barnett, There's not gonna be any crabs here before the middle of the season. Cold as this winter got, the ice has sucked the big ones out of the mud and killed 'em. Let's take a hundred pots and go down to Texas and look it over.

Sherwood Moore and Leonard Shorter, "Jess" and "Dick," in Miss Nora's store.

He said, Sure, we'll go to Texas.

So first we went to Crisfield and bought a hundred crab-pots—piled them up and anchored them down on this fiberglass boat Grant had bought a month before.

While we're shopping, Grant said, Here, let's pick up a couple of these crab tongs.

Whadda we want them for? I asked, but he bought a couple anyway.

We took off, trailing the rig down to Texas, going the

southern way through 2,100 miles of farm country, keeping out of the mountains. All along the way, people stared at us trailing that boat with those pots all piled up on it. They guessed everything you can think of, but nobody knew what those pots were.

Whatcha got there? one guy asked. Chicken coops?

Nope, they're crab-pots, I said.

Why, you can't catch no crabs 'round here, he told us.

Stopping for gas a little farther along, a guy eyed our stuff and asked, Whadda y'll catch in them wire baskets?

Crabs, I said, and he looked at me the same as if I'd said bear.

Even near the water down there, it was the same. One place by the Gulf of Mexico, an old guy about eighty sat fishing.

What kinda cages ye got there? he asked.

They're crab traps, I told him.

You're the onliest man with crab traps I ever seen in my life.

***

We drove straight through, taking turns napping. Forty-eight hours later we were in San Antonio. After all those miles cross-country, we hit San Antonio in thick rush-hour traffic. We inched along this four-lane street to an intersection, where a cop directed traffic.

He stopped us there at a traffic light and yelled over, Hey buddy, where you going with them crab-pots?

Brownsville, Texas, I said.

Good enough, said the cop, waving us on.

I told him, You're the onliest man knew what we had.

***

We got a motel room in San Antonio and unhitched the boat. At a liquor store across the street, we bought a bottle of Jack Daniels, then went uptown to have a drink. A lot of those places down there, you carried your own. You couldn't buy a drink, but you paid for a glass of ice as much as a drink would cost. Coming back that night, we lost the motel where our boat was at, but about two o'clock we found it, hooked up, and took off for Brownsville without ever using the room.

Next day we went to a sporting goods store and bought our licenses—$12 each for the season. The first week down there, we worked this bay off the Rio Grande River by Padre Island—water so salt our arms looked white at the end of the day. We had to scrape the salt off us, and they'd had some rain that year. In a real dry year, water got so briny it killed everything.

We caught nice, big crabs. First time I reached in the cull box for one of those Texas crabs, it reached back up at me, claws clear to my upper arm.

I said, Grant, pass me one of them crab tongs. You were right about them.

We caught $2,000 worth of crabs that first week. We decided we could make a bundle on our own instead of crabbing for somebody else. A packer had a warehouse on the border and a picking house in Matamoros, Mexico. Crabs sold for twenty-five cents a pound straight, no culling. He said he'd take all the crabs we caught, but he'd never seen nobody catch more than six or seven bushels a day. The first time me and Grant showed up with our catch, he couldn't believe his eyes.

That's when I flew home for my own pickup and bought another boat. I couldn't trail a 32-foot wooden boat like *Miss Wendy* over the road, so I needed something I could move around quicker. I went down to Crisfield and bought a 21-foot T-Craft, a 150-horsepower Mercury outboard, and two hundred more pots. I stacked a hundred and fifty on my boat and pickup—not so high and wide as to be illegal, but I went through some tight spots without much clearance. Donnie

Bowman put my other fifty pots on his truck and tailgated me down to Texas just to have a look.

We only stopped at truck stops to get gas and have something to eat. My Chevrolet wouldn't go over fifty mile-per-hour pulling that boat. When we got to Georgia, it dropped two or three cylinders and couldn't get up any speed at all on those little hills. On my CB radio I found a dealer in LaGrange, Georgia and drove on into town, leaving my rig with Donnie. The mechanic went right to work on her. He took the oil stick out of her.

What's she look like? I asked.

She's pretty inside, he said, checking the stick. You been changing the oil, ain't ya?

I said, There's never been a wrench on her.

She had 80,000 miles on her then.

He got her right, but in Alabama I had to go over this big tall bridge and I didn't think she was gonna make it. She got down to thirty mile-an-hour, using everything she had into her. If it had been another hundred feet to the top, I don't know what would've happened.

***

Counting me and Grant, for two hundred miles of coastline, there weren't seven crabbers, and they just knew to throw the pot overboard. We worked the Intercoastal Waterway, behind Padre Island. Donnie stayed and helped till I got my pots set out, then he left. After that, it was a job, but I could fish two hundred a day by myself. We only had to cull out sponge crabs. Every week I went into town and sent money home by Western Union.

Before long, we found a little motel by a marina in Port Mansfield. Me and Grant took a room and moved up there. I could see my boat tied up in the harbor from my window. A fishhouse stood right there, where we could get bait, run by a fella named Joe.

Chapter 30

PORT MANSFIELD

When we got to Port Mansfield, Texas, a local who did a little crabbing said, You boys only got a couple weeks of good crabbing before they leave here and go out in the Gulf. You ought to know there ain't much crabbing left this time of year.

I said, That's pretty good, I bought a new boat and drove 2,100 miles and only gonna get to crab two weeks.

I knew better than that, though, 'cause you could see this was crabbing ground. But the local boys cared more about fishing and shrimping, and never paid too much notice to crabbing. When it came to that two weeks, they pulled up and put their crab-pots on the bank. We went out, dropping pots here and there, pulling up crabs. Any bay area like that, you know they've got crabs in there. I'd start dropping pots by the time we got out of the marina. The water was only four or five feet deep. We weren't gone no time and coming back in with plenty of crabs, half of them those old big ones. We caught

Tied up by the Port Mansfield fishhouse are the boats of shrimpers and fishermen Beer Breath, Big Pete, Skip and Butch.

enough market fish in our pots to swap for bait. We traded them for alewives, catfish, anything. When we got all our rig out, we brought in 2,000 or 2,500 pounds of crabs every day. The locals stared at us, 'cause we were strange to them. They stood there on that bank for one month, they did, and watched us bring those crabs in.

One would say, Where'd you get them crabs at?

Not knowing the names of places around there, I'd point, I don't know—up the river—on that other side there.

They thought crabs must be moving back where they always crabbed. They didn't know nothing about how crabs move here and there. Finally, they'd seen enough from us and said they were gonna get their crab-pots.

One crabber we called the Cadillac Kid. You saw lots of Cadillacs on the road down there. He had this big, white sedan towing a little trailer, so he wouldn't have to carry his catch in his Cadillac.

I was out fishing my pots one day when the Cadillac Kid sailed up and asked, Can I put my pots over alongside of yours?

I said, Yes indeed honey, help yourself. Put 'em right in here anywhere you want.

When I told him to come on, he dropped his pots all in the middle of mine, each one in my row. He caught about 150 pounds while I got 2,000. How it happened, they made pots down there that weren't worth nothing. They didn't have rebar on them. Without rebars' weight, pots jump on the bottom with any wind blowing and crabs aren't gonna go in there. The chamber wasn't steep enough either. A crab could find its way out. They didn't have zinc in their pots to keep salt from eating them They had black vinyl pots and any amount of crabs would cut that vinyl, then salt ate the pot.

***

All kinds of drifters passed through the motel there at

the harbor, going in and out of town. They worked two or three days on a boat, then you didn't see them no more. They looked like these cowboys you see on television.

The ones with small bait-shrimp boats didn't drift as much. They stayed on in the motel. Bait-shrimping was a big thing, but they didn't work too hard either. One guy called Beer Breath never left the harbor—just dragged back and forth four times and had his jag of grass shrimp for the day.

A shrimper came walking down the dock one day with this gal he'd picked up, telling her about his shrimp boat he was gonna take her on.

She walked along pointing out all the big boats tied up there, asking him, Is that yours?

Nope.

Is that yours?

Nope.

When they got to the end, he said, That's mine.

Where?

Down there, he said pointing to this little 16-foot plywood skiff he worked.

***

Others staying at the motel fished a lot of trout. Gill nets weren't legal, so they strung lines made up like trotlines between poles. The tide hardly raised at all down there, and they strung the line just above the water. Trout or flounder came up and took the bait. Sometimes they went fishing up in the bayous and stayed two or three days.

We met a trout fisherman named Guy who said, I got a camp about twenty miles up in the bayou. Why don't you all come up fishing with me for the night.

Me and Grant wanted to take everything in, so we said, Okay.

Sailing up there looked just like going up from the mouth of the Blackwater River. In Texas and Louisiana they called them bayous, but they weren't much different from our rivers and marsh. Around the edge of dark we landed at this shanty Guy had up there on stilts—a nice place with a generator to run his lights and everything.

Flicking on this outside light he had rigged, he said, Let me show you boys how to catch fish.

Pretty soon we could see the trout—swarms of them—coming to the light. We caught the devil out of them hook-and-lining, and had fun doing it. It's not often you can do something you enjoy that much and make money at the same time.

***

The way they sold their fish, the fishermen iced them down when they caught them. When they came in to Port Mansfield to land them, the same guys cleaned them. The fishhouse looked like a big warehouse with a wharf. Workbenches stood inside for those boys. They snipped around the fishes' eyes and split and gutted them, then threw them into a box of ice without scaling them. Those guys walked all around that fishhouse barefoot, with all those fish bones on the floor. They were the toughest people I ever saw on feet. Sand briars grew between the fishhouse and our motel, but walking across those briars didn't faze them.

They worked with nothing but shorts on. We wore waders and every darn thing. Humidity wasn't high. A hundred degrees felt like eighty does at home.

I usually left the harbor about sunup. Before I shoved off one morning, a couple of those fishermen came down the dock early, all dressed up—cowboy boots shined, 10-gallon hats cocked back.

I said, Man, where you all goin' this morning?

We're fixin' to go to San Antone, they said. Goin' to San Antone for a week. Come on, go with us.

I can't, I said, I got to fish these pots.

Those boys fished three or four days, making good money. A little skiff is all they needed in that shallow water. Before the week was out, they had all the money they needed and were gone a week, then here they come back again.

I wish now I'd gone to San Antone with them. I never did go to Mickey Gillie's either, where they had a mechanical bull to ride. I don't know why not. I tried everything else. I did get a couple pair of cowboy boots, though, at a store in McAllen--Mack Allen, they called it. They were good boots—buy one pair and you got another free.

Me and Grant did go to Mexico. There's no ride like riding in a Mexican taxi. Back then, they had old cars like we'd throw on a junk heap. We rode with one guy, hair down his back, talking Mexican at us over his shoulder, flying down dirt roads. We saw four sets of headlights coming at us and he swerved and dodged, foxtails flying by outside the windows, ooga-ooga horns and bells and car horns blowing. I don't know how we got through, but we did.

I never took more than twenty dollars over the border with me, so if somebody got that they weren't getting much. Grant didn't worry. We went in one bar—him tall and blond—women got all over him like termites.

I said, Grant, they're goin' in your pockets.

He said, T'hell with it.

Wy-Leto is what they called me.

It cost two-cents to get back across the bridge into the States. We took a taxi back once and between us, we just did have the four-cents we needed for the bridge.

I said, Grant, what're we gonna do? We can't pay for this taxi.

He said, Don't worry. When he starts to slow down, we'll jump out and run.

I said, Man, we're gonna get killed.

Grant said, Don't worry. When I say, 'Let's go,' just

jump and run.

As we saw the Rio Grande, the driver started to slow down. We jumped out the doors and ran like hell, the driver back there cussing us. Not that we could understand a word, but we got his drift.

Next time we went over the border, we took more care with our money, but as our taxi got near the bridge, this police car came roaring up and stopped us. They got me up against the taxi on one side and Grant on the other. They searched him and me and searched the taxi. I didn't know what they were looking for.

I.D., the cop with me said.

I had my driver's license, but Grant didn't have nothing.

The cop on his side came around waving towards Grant, Who he is?

Grant Barnett, I said.

If I'd said, I don't know who the hell he is, Grant would have been gone. I had that to throw up to him—how I'd saved him from a Mexican jail.

***

The fishhouse manager Joe had a son Ronnie, twelve or thirteen years old. When Texas schools let out, Ronnie wanted to go crabbing with me. I used to put eight or ten pots here, eight or ten in another place, scatter them around a little bit to locate the crabs. Ronnie's first day aboard, I'd been working up the bay there when I hit some crabs in pots set down below. So I pulled up a load of upper pots and carried them down below to put them overboard. I left the engine in gear and got up on the side of the boat to snip the pots loose from where I had them tied down. The T-Craft didn't have much washboard. I got tangled in the rubber strip on some pot and my boot slipped and I went overboard. When I felt myself falling, I jumped clear so I wouldn't hit against the boat. We were in the channel, the only deep water in the Intercostal, where all the big barges come through. If I tried to catch myself, I might knock myself out on the side of my boat.

That boy left aboard didn't know what to do. I kicked off my boots so they wouldn't pull me down, then swam after the boat. He needed to take her out of gear, so he wouldn't pull off and leave me.

I hollered, See that black knob on your left?

He got it into neutral, like I told him, but the tide was running. He was drifting away and I couldn't catch up. I kept paddling, hollering to him how to put it in reverse.

Afraid he'd back into me, I told him, Move the stick back *real easy*.

He did and, when he had me back aboard, that boy felt ten feet tall. That stuff happens on the water. Young like I was then, it doesn't bother you.

Those boots I lost were white boots we bought for about $20 a pair at the fishhouse. Before going to Texas, we never had seen white boots. We brought them up here to the Eastern Shore when we came home and now everybody in the world's got a pair of white rubber boots.

***

When I first got to Port Mansfield, Joe had looked at me for about three weeks, watching with the others, then told me, If these darn boys ain't goin' out there, I'm gonna go out and catch some of them crabs.

I said, There's plenty of room out there.

He worked a big plyboard scow 25-foot long, square in the bow, with an outboard on it. He came to lay his lines alongside mine, and his pretty little daughter came out helping him—this little gal steering, wearing nothing but a sombrero and a yellow bikini. Here she was, brown as a berry, shaking his pots out. I was running over his lines with sweat running off of me all day long.

***

Grant wasn't in Port Mansfield long before he got restless and went back to Maryland, but I stayed. I didn't need hardly any money down there, so I sent most all of it home. I went to Western Union one morning and wired what I had. Later in the day, Louella called the fishhouse to let me know Daddy was in the hospital and it could go either way.

Joe said, You need any money? Whadda you want?

I said, About $300.

He peeled off $300 and handed it to me. I flew out of Brownsville about an hour later. I was home three or four days when Daddy turned it around, so I flew back to Texas. I'd left my boat at the fishhouse and when I got back, Ronnie had put a new coat of copper on her bottom.

***

Me and Joe went out looking for bait sometimes. There were schools of alewives down there—they called them pogeys.

We spotted a school of them and he said, I can catch 'em with my cast net.

I said, I'll get 'em there to you.

He had one of these cast nets you hook around your wrist and throw like a lasso. I ran into a bunch of them pogeys and slacked off. He got up and I thought he was gonna fall off. He had a tennis shoe on him a foot long. He planted them feet and swung that net around and tossed it so it would spread out and settle on the bottom. Then he snatched it real quick. Man, he had a half-bushel every lick. I never did try that cast net; I knew I'd fall overboard.

We caught mullet too. They're hard to catch, 'cause they jump out of the water. After you catch them, they're harder to keep in the basket than crabs, but they make good bait.

*C*hapter 31

SUMMER IN TEXAS

When school let out, I flew home from Texas again. I'd already closed the Salisbury shop and Louella and the kids wanted to see Texas, so I drove everybody down for the summer. Grant decided then to get his two boys and go back too, so I put my dogs, Charlie and Beazley, in the back of Grant's pickup. I drove Louella's car with her, our three kids, and Wendy's tabby cat, Twinkle.

When we stopped for gas in this one town, Charlie and Beazley jumped out to take a leak and kept on going, like they knew every inch of the territory. Grant didn't have much patience, but the kids were wailing and he dared not leave. After driving around an hour, we found the dogs and got them back in Grant's truck. Wendy had a collar on Twinkle, so she could walk him at rest stops.

It's hard to believe, but when I got back close to LaGrange, Georgia again, Louella's car broke down. The dealer we took it to elbowed us around, trying to get a load of money out of us. I called Louella's brother Steve, an auto executive in Detroit. After Steve got a hold of that dealer, he put us up in a motel, gave us a loaner to drive, and halved the repair charge he'd estimated.

Nothing else went wrong till we got to Houston and stopped to get something to eat. When we came out, Twinkle had wiggled out the window and we never did find him.

***

I rented a house on a little circle right behind the motel where I'd been staying. There was a swimming pool across from us, just right for Wendy, who swam like a dolphin. She made friends with another girl there, Sherry. Robert was young then, but Willie came on to work with me.

Every morning we went out, Charlie swam along with us from where we pushed off to the mouth of the marina, then he turned around and paddled back home. When we got back in the harbor, he'd come aboard. If mullet were jumping, he'd stand in the tail end of that boat trying to catch them. It took him a month, but he finally got one.

They didn't have retrievers down there and couldn't believe how mine went overboard. One fella had a bad dog, some big mean kind. Charlie and that dog met, walking towards each other. Charlie could tell he was bad, so when they got close, he folded his legs and got down on his belly. The mean dog went by, then reached around and bit Charlie's backside. That did it. Charlie didn't want to fight that dog, but when he got bit like that, he whirled around and lit into him. Charlie knocked that dog overboard, then had him where he wanted him.

***

Two brothers we came to like a lot, Butch and Skip, stayed in this little community where we rented. They didn't have much to say at first. I'd say hello and they'd say hello. After they saw how many crabs I brought in, they talked a little more and we got to be good friends. They drove a car, but before long got a pickup like mine and we put wooden sides on her. Then one day I'd haul crabs to Brownsville and they'd haul the next.

When we first got to Port Mansfield, nobody there ate crabs. They called crabs the buzzards of the sea, which I guess they are. I had some seasoning I always carried with me when I went anywhere. We steamed up some crabs with that seasoning and everybody started coming over—couldn't believe how good they tasted.

Certain time of the season, ninety percent of the catch was peelers, but the packer put them in with everything else. That's when I thought to myself, this guy doesn't know nothing about crabs. The old gal who ran the gas pumps at the marina had been up north and liked soft crabs, so I saved some out for her and for us. I had a mess of them in my refrigerator and this Texan saw me take one out to fry up and couldn't believe I'd eat it shell and all.

***

One morning I told Willie, We'll go out in the Gulf and try eight or ten pots to see if there's some crabs out there.

There wasn't no need to, 'cause we caught plenty in the Intercoastal where we were, but we went out anyway and set a few pots. The water's real clear and blue after you get out into the Gulf past Padre Island—clear enough to see the bottom. We baited a couple pots and threw them overboard. Five sharks' fins popped up. One old hammerhead big as the T-Craft came circling around, eyeing us. Willie's hand was in a bucket of fish, all bloody from baiting pots.

He said, Let's get out of here before folks have to call me Lefty from now on.

I said, Yeah, let's get these pots up and get back in the Intercoastal.

Locals said sharks schooled the thickest that year they'd ever been. You could look and see ten or fifteen at a time out in the Gulf. A few would come into the Intercoastal, but not many. Sometimes those boys fishing trotlines would bring up nothing but fish heads. Helicopters flew up and down Padre Island beaches all day telling people to get out of the water.

Those shrimpers that came in to Port Mansfield, when they caught a shark, they cut him up and skinned him out and saved the jaws. They had shark jaws that gaped as big around as basket tops.

***

Something else that grew big down there was raccoons. Me and Louella were driving one evening from Port Mansfield to Raymondsville when a couple 'coons ran out in the road.

Louella hadn't been in Texas long and she said, Look out! Don't hit those dogs.

I said, They're no dogs, they're 'coons.

She said, There's no 'coons in the world that big.

That's what they were, though. You could go down to that little restaurant at the marina early in the morning and there'd be twenty of these forty- or fifty-pound 'coons in the dumpster, real horses they were. One of the drifters knew I trapped. When I'd gone back home, he caught some up and sent the hides to Maryland for me to see what they'd bring. He sent me coyotes, too. I couldn't do nothing with either of them, though, 'cause the fur from that warm climate wasn't good.

***

Grant left Texas again around the middle of summer. He broke a throttle cable on his motor on a Thursday. Friday evening I found him pulling his boat up and I thought he was putting it on the wheels to go have it fixed.

I asked him, Where you gonna take her?

I'm goin' home, he said.

What're you goin' home for?

Goin' home.

I don't know; something didn't strike him right. You couldn't keep Grant down.

When time came for school to start, Louella took the kids and drove back home, so I didn't have Willie to help me anymore. After I worked by myself for a week, this guy came walking down the dock, maybe thirty years old, dressed in jeans and a T-shirt.

He said, Hey buddy, don't need a deck hand do you?

I said, I don't know. Things are kinda tight here now—not making much.

I'll work for anything, he said.

How about $20 a day?

Good.

He knew how to handle crab-pots, so evidently he'd done that before. All I had to do was steer and hook. I kept him on for the rest of my time down there, but never once saw him eat. Not every morning, but a lot of them, he'd come aboard and pull three or four pots and break down with dry heaves.

As I got ready to go home, he said, Captain, when you leave, could I have that little cooler you got there?

I said, Yes indeedy.

I had a little foam cooler that held six cans. I put six beers in as I was leaving and packed it up with ice. He was a happy boy. I didn't know till then, but come to find out he slept in an old car, and there I was with a whole house to myself.

***

My pots looked as good the day I left as the day I started. For some reason they didn't foul up down there like they do around Chesapeake Bay. I sold them for six dollars apiece to Joe and left them overboard with whatever was in them. He knew where to find them, so all he had to do was go fish them. I'd paid ten dollars each for them, but those pots didn't owe me nothing.

***

The day I left was Butch and Skip's turn to haul crabs. I was loading everything, packing up. We had about a fifteen mile drive out from our houses to the main road, nearly like from Elliotts Island to Vienna.

I told them, If I get loaded before you get back, I'll probably meet you along the road.

That's what happened. They had my check for me. They wanted me to stay down there, they did. I looked over at this one old boy and tears were rolling down his cheeks.

***

Driving back home to Maryland, I kept $500 cash in my pocket in case I got broke down or something. When I got tired and sleepy, I pulled over in a rest area and tied a dog to each door handle. Nobody ever bothered me.

Those dogs hated Volkswagens. A VW running on the highway had a whistle to it. Charlie and Beazley rode in the back of the pickup. When a Volkswagen passed us, both those dogs jumped up barking and raising the devil.

I got back home in time for ducking.

Chapter 32

THE GOAT

The old Nanticoke Inn was headquarters for everybody who worked anywhere around Vienna—the farmers and watermen and trappers. That's before it got redone, back when it was still called The Goat. In gunning seasons, all the deer and duck hunters from the western shore came in the Goat too. Hardly any trouble ever broke out between locals and anybody who knew how to act. Of course, somebody who didn't act right straggled in sometimes.

In those days, Route 50 ran right past the Nanticoke Inn, just a few feet beyond the side door. A gang of bikers roared up and stopped in one day thinking they were bad. Ray Moore was leaving when one of the bikers got up and spit on him. Ray packed a wallop and he popped that guy one time and sent him flying backwards, hard enough to break the door off the hinges. Door and biker ended up outside on the ground. Ray just stood inside there, fist cocked, and looked around at the rest of them.

Who's next? he asked.

They all drank up quick, jammed out the empty doorway, and headed on down the road.

***

Another fella named William used to hang in there a lot. William had a short fuse. A stranger came in one night who couldn't hold his drinks and was needling people up and down the bar. William stood down to the end, drinking his beer, minding his own business. I was clear of it, shooting shuffleboard, but I thought to myself, when that character gets to William it'll be the end of the line. Before long I heard a crash and didn't even have to look up from my game. I knew exactly what happened.

***

Before we got shuffleboard, a couple pinball machines stood against the outside wall. My man, the Duke, who fished with us, had a temper on him sometimes too. He was playing pinball one day and tilted his machine.

Dammit, he said, I need my money back.

Nothin' doin', the owner told him, you done that yourself.

The Duke gave the pinball machine a big shove. That machine went flying, shattering the glass, busted through the window, flipped over outside, and crashed upside-down in Route 50.

***

The Goat had been built about the same time as the power plant in Vienna, with rooms to rent upstairs to construction workers. By the time I came along, the upstairs had been turned into sort of a game room. We played poker up there many a night. Sometimes, when we were drift-netting in the Nanticoke River, we played till the tide was right, or we slipped back for a few hands between drifts. Generally we agreed when we sat down, we'll play till such-and-such a time, according to the tide.

When we stayed ashore in rough weather, play might start in the afternoon and go all night. Two or three of us would drift in and decide to get up a game. Then we started dropping dimes in the payphone, calling our regulars.

We're getting up a game, we said. Come on by.

This old gal Irene who tended bar had a time getting us to stop playing and come down so she could close up. We played regular Five Card Stud or High-Low Split, sometimes Seven Card Chicago, low spade in the hole or regular. There weren't no one dollar bills on that upstairs table, there was some serious money. You take five or six guys betting five or ten or twenty dollars a pop, pots averaged two or three hundred. Some pots easily built to a thousand or fifteen hundred dollar.

We had dart boards up there too. We got a team together and joined a league, traveling around the Shore playing other bars' teams. Some nights I couldn't miss, but next round I wouldn't be able to hit the board. I shot shuffleboard the same way.

***

My neighbor, Gorman Gray, patrolled around the Island a lot, but didn't go up the road as far as Vienna too often. He mostly drove back and forth from Poplar Island back home, just a couple miles. I met him one evening on the upper end of his loop, and flagged him down.

Gorman Gray landed oysters at Elliott Brothers Seafood around 1960.

I said, Park her at Poplar Island, Gorman, and I'll carry you up to Vienna with me.

He did that and we went on up to the Goat and got all drunked up. Gorman wasn't comfortable being out so far from home and coming back late—about three in the morning.

We got down around Savannah Lake and he asked, Will you get me home, Abbott?

Don't worry, Gorman. Abbott'll get you home.

You sure?

Don't worry. Abbott'll get you home.

About that time, I nodded off. Next thing I knew, reeds were flying and cattails hitting the windshield. We came to rest in the ditch tilted about 45-degrees.

Gorman's leaning over me asking, What're we gonna do, Abbott?

I said, I don't know about you, but I'm goin' back to sleep. When somebody comes along, I'll climb in with 'em.

Well, said Gorman, I'm gonna walk down and get my car.

This from a guy who never crossed the road to the store afoot. But he climbed out and set off for his car, a good five miles away. He must have run part way. He covered the length of the marsh road from Savannah to Poplar Island and got back to pick me up before first light.

***

Back in those days I was the only one on the Island road at that hour. We only had one-way traffic, with pull-offs for cars crossing the marsh from the other direction. You could see lights from anybody coming a mile away. Between the end of ducking season and the first of crabbing, you never saw a strange car pass, even during the day. In the middle of the night, I had it all to myself. Sometimes I used every bit of it.

I got near Langralls Island one night and nodded off. I woke up going off to my left, cut my wheel a little too much, started off the other side, then cut again a little too far. On the third cut, I hit a tree at such an angle, I clipped the CB antenna off the top of my cab.

One Saturday night, when I was driving my little red '66 Mustang, I went to town for a while. I wasn't planning to be too late, because I had a fishing party coming down from Baltimore early Sunday morning.

Just after daylight, one of these guys knocked on my front door asking Louella for me.

He's not home, she said. Did you pass a little red car in the ditch anywhere on your way down?

The first guy shook his head no, but another one spoke up and said, I didn't know it was a car, but I think I saw somethin' red out in the marsh.

Louella sent my 6-wheeler up with them to pull me out and we went fishing.

***

When I got in trouble, it usually came from not having sense enough to stay put in Vienna. I was so used to starting and ending my day at the Goat, I reported my pickup stolen once when I found myself there afoot.

What happened was, I left the Goat early one day to meet a couple guys in Cambridge—Lindy Pritchett for one, and a Parks who married my cousin. We had a couple drinks at the bar in the Quality Court Motel, then went over to the Legion, where we ran into Grant Barnett and more guys we knew. We had some ginger brandy at the Legion, then Lindy wanted to go to Salisbury. Me and Parks rode down with Lindy and had a couple at a hotel bar before heading back to Cambridge to the Quality. Parks lived in Cambridge, but said he'd carry me back to Vienna, so we went on down Route 50 and he dropped me off.

By that time, the Goat had been closed for hours. I looked around outside there and didn't see my pickup. Across the road, a state trooper and a deputy sheriff were sitting in their squad cars.

I walked over to the trooper and said, Man, I just come back from Cambridge and my pickup's missin'.

He said, Anybody else with you tonight?

I said, Yeah, my two buddies, but they've gone on home now.

Who were you out with? he asked.

I said, With a couple guys, then we ran into Grant

Barnett.

He knew Grant and said, Call and see if he's seen your truck.

He carried me to the payphone at Bunky Bell's service station. I drew a blank and couldn't think of Grant's number. There was a phone book right there, but I couldn't focus my eyes on the numbers and didn't want to make a show of myself, so I dialed Louella.

She said, Where in the world you at?

I'm outside Bunky's.

She wasn't too happy with me, but I told her my truck had gone missing and what was going on and she got me Grant's number.

He picked up the phone and I asked him, Grant, you seen my truck tonight?

He said, Yeah, she's at the Quality Court.

I knew then what I'd done, but I just told the cop, Grant seen my truck at the Quality Court.

He said, Come on, get in here.

I climbed in his squad car and he powered her up Route 50 to Cambridge fast as she'd go, siren wailing and light flashing. He about rattled my teeth out. When we got to the motel, my pickup sat parked outside the bar, right where I'd left her.

The trooper said, Let me go first and check her out.

I said, Okay, go right ahead. That's a good idea.

He got his flashlight out and stalked all around her. I went stalking right around behind him.

I told him, I think she's all right.

She looked okay to him too, but he opened the door and shone his light around inside double-checking.

Are you okay on gas? he asked.

I might be.

He checked the gauge and said, You're low. There's a

gas station right across the highway there. You get your gas and go on home.

I went over and got my ten dollars' worth of gas and headed home. I was wore out.

***

Another night I got stopped, a trooper pulled me over and wanted me to take a sobriety test.

Let's see you walk a straight line, he said.

I told him, That's no test. Why don't you ask me to stand on my head?

I flipped upside down and did a hand-stand and he said, Aw, go on home.

*C*hapter 33

THREE OVERHAULS

When I first started guiding, I used to leave a skiff-load of decoys tied up on the riverside all through gunning season and never lost one, but people have gone decoy-crazy since then. Somebody broke into the shed at my clubhouse one fall and took the best decoys we had, some that had belonged in the duPont family for a long time. We lost 180 Madison Mitchells. I guess whoever did that knew they'd struck something.

A little while later, an investigator from the sheriff's office called me up and said, I think I got your decoys back.

Man-oh-man, I said, that's great.

. . .But, he went on, we gotta take a right good ride to get 'em.

I don't care how far. We'll go.

We drove clear to Havre de Grace, where a pawnshop had all different kinds of decoys, but not mine. I put little plugs into a bunch of mine. I drilled a little teeny-tiny hole, plugged them, and put paint on it. I could identify them with that if I had any doubt. One I plugged kind of leaned over in the water when I threw him overboard. I'd know my own if I ran into them. Some I'd had in my hand forty years. I never did find any of them. I guess some would be worth thousands of dollars today. We found out later that the decoys the detective took me to had been stolen out of Delaware.

When they broke into our shed we had three dozen goose decoys and three dozen black ducks. They only took half. I guess they couldn't carry them all. Next deer season, darn if they didn't come back and get the rest of them and more besides.

They stole a 25-horsepower outboard motor, but they probably did me a favor taking that. Even brand new, most of the time she only ran on one cylinder. If the last cylinder ever gave out, I'd have been broke down in the river. On a rough winter day, that's no place to be without a motor. If they hadn't stolen that sumbitch, it could've taken my life. I used to go in cold weather, wind blowing. It didn't make no difference what, I'd go.

***

One cold January morning, I'd run some of my club out gunning on the Nanticoke before daylight. We didn't stay long. It breezed up, so we got our ducks and came on in. We'd been shooting black ducks.

One member named Bill said, I'd like to get some bluebills.

I said, Come on, go with me.

He followed me down the road and across the Island to the Lower Creek. I'd built a blind off the south shore, just outside the mouth of the harbor. It was blowing pretty good by the time we got there—about two o'clock. Wind was out of the north, not far from thirty miles-an-hour, but I put some wet ones out in those days. This blind stood off the point, close to the harbor's mouth. I put my skiff overboard and put Bill in the blind with an Island teenager. We were allowed about twenty bluebills at that time, and they had a big shoot. The temperature kept dropping. I saw the wind tilting that blind and thought it time to get them out.

I had a ramp up to the door of the blind that I ran my skiff onto—a 16-foot aluminum skiff with a 20-horsepower Johnson on her. I had the devil of a time running in there. To hit it right, I had to go in head-to, but the wind was blowing her off. I circled around and struck the runway as hard as she could go, then cut her off quick. In case we needed to leave in a hurry, I stood holding the boat. If I'd tied the rope, I might not have got her unfastened. The blind was rocking and every drop of spray that flew froze.

I said, Boys, I think we better pack it up and go. It's getting bad.

Old Bill said, If Wylie says it's bad, it's bad. Let's go.

We got the decoys collected up and went ashore. When we got to the parking lot, there was Junior Willey waiting for me.

He said, Wylie, Chip Chew and another gunner called for help. They radioed the clubhouse from Duck Island, they can't get their boat goin'.

Cell phones weren't around then, but luckily one of their gunners kept radio equipment at Chip's father's clubhouse for business. I got back in my skiff and the boy jumped in with me. We hadn't gone three hundred yards when here came another skiff headed upwind for the Island. We didn't even know they were out there—a skiff full of Baltimore judges and lawyers from the Myrtle Gray Gunning Club—five head in a 16-foot aluminum skiff going into the wind. Their high-sided skiff should have been okay, but they bunched up too far forward. Water was coming right over her bow and you could see she was gonna sink. Just as the motor drowned out, they got her turned into the bank and started jumping ashore.

I said, We gotta get them 'fore we go to Duck Island. They'll freeze to death 'fore we get back.

I ran my skiff into the shore and they climbed aboard without saying a word. Between the spray freezing on them and the water they'd taken on, they were soaked up to their knees and their hands turned purple. They brought their guns along and we left their skiff and decoys on the bank. Now I had two head more in my skiff than what sank them, but the weight helped me 'cause I balanced them right. Their weight held my boat down and kept it from bouncing all over the place. I didn't have far to carry them back to the dock and put them out, but I noticed in passing that my blind was leaning worse.

***

After getting those five ashore, me and the boy set out again for the three mile run to the next two, Chip and his friend. Running downwind, it took us about an hour to Duck Island, wind blowing so hard the sea came up over the back end of the skiff. When we got there, we found this heavy old wooden skiff of theirs hung on the bank. They had it chocked into the bank, the bow wedged in there and the motor's lower unit frozen into the clay. The tide had left them and she froze there and they couldn't get her off. With four of us, we wiggled her loose and shoved her overboard off the bank. They started up and ran about a hundred yards, rounding the point into the wind. Then their motor cut out and never would make another toot. They started drifting south, away from the Island, and we tossed them a towline. Then we had a 20-horsepower Johnson bucking into thirty-mile-an-hour wind, towing a big old heavy wooden boat with two men and all their decoys and gear—the same as dragging a big log through the water. I was afraid we didn't have enough.

I reached in my pocket and said, Here's my pocket knife. When I tell you to cut this sumbitch line, you cut her, 'cause I ain't gonna let her drag me down river. We'll go back and get the men off and to hell with that old boat.

In the end we never had to cut her loose. We drug it all up to the harbor. It probably took us three hours to beat our way back, colder than death, but we got the men and boat and gear all back in the harbor. We had to roll those two boys out of the boat. In those days, Chip had long hair and great long icicles hung off him. He ain't forgot that trip.

Chip told me later, We thought we'd had it. The wind

– 204 –

Chip Chew arrived at his lodge from Duck Island frost-covered.

was whistling around us and waves crashing. We had a bottle along and decided we shouldn't freeze to death with a full bottle. We were putting it in us when all of a sudden the light struck us.

That was my flashlight I had with me. That trip was the coldest I ever been in my life. When we got to the harbor that last time, I could barely get out of the skiff. I had to pick my leg up with my two hands to put it on the side of the boat and haul myself onto the dock.

***

I never walked into Gittle Gray's Upper Store till eight o'clock that night, and I'd been going since way before daylight. Icicles hung from my hair down into my collar. I looked white as chalk from head to toe, spray frozen all over me. I hadn't eaten all day, but didn't want to go home carrying all that ice. I just wanted to get next to the big, hot stove Gittle had middle way of that store. When I went in, three or four Islanders were still sitting around with Gittle, all staring at me coming in the door.

Gittle said, My lord, son, where you been? You ain't been out in that river today, bad as it is.

I said, I made three overhauls this evening, rescuing duck hunters.

Gittle spit chewing tobacco into his spittoon and said, You gonna be drownded some day. Come on up here by the fire.

I told them all what happened, then I left a puddle

melted there on Gittle's floor and went home for my supper.

***

Next morning when I went down to the harbor, the old wooden boat I towed from Duck Island had sunk right there at the wharf. I ran down to the point and bailed out the lawyers' skiff and towed it back. Nothing remained of my blind.

Bill, the member in my blind after bluebills, didn't live to see the next season, but he had a big shoot that day. And those other boys I brought ashore that night respect me. They knew they'd been in trouble.

I've had to help hunt a couple times for guys lost on the marsh and I don't ever want to do that again.

Chapter 34

COLD NIGHTS AND A HOT DAY

I was sleeping about ten o'clock one cold January night when the phone woke me up, Tommy Tyler calling from Henrys Crossroads.

Wylie, he said, I need your help if you'll go.

Whadda you gonna do? I asked him.

He said, There's three guys I know went duckin' up Ther'fer Creek. Something's happened to 'em and I can't get a marine policeman anywhere in the whole state of Maryland.

Are you sure they're still out? I asked, hoping for a way out.

Yeah, I know where they're at. They stopped by home here before putting overboard at Lewis Wharf, heading across the river. They never came back here, so I rode down to the wharf and their pickup's still there.

He was talking about a creek that runs through the marsh across from Lewis Wharf, a good ten miles up the road above the Island, then across the Nanticoke River into Wicomico County.

I said, Gawd-a-mighty no, Tommy, I don't want to go, but if it'll save a life we'll go. Meet me at my boat. We'll have to break some ice.

The creeks and river had all iced up and Tommy knew I had my fiberglass T-Craft tied up in Wapermander Creek. I used the T-Craft for my club after getting her in 1977. I could break more ice in that fiberglass boat than in my wooden boat, plus I had a 200-horsepower Mercury on her.

Tommy met me about forty-five minutes later at the boat and we set off. We broke ice two and three inches deep all the way from the time we started down Wapermander and crossed the Nanticoke up into Rewastico Creek to Ther'fer Creek. New ice had been making all day. Luckily, the wind wasn't blowing much and a big full moon shone. I could see ahead pretty good, which helped. I'd gun my motor to get my speed up and ram the ice. When we got hung up, we rocked the boat back and forth to break her loose again. I could see well enough not to barrel-ass into any chunks floating in the river and tear my boat up. When we got in Rewastico Creek, we made that turn there into Ther'fer and ran up about a mile, right in a line across the river from Lewis Wharf. We found the duck blind and three gunners, right where Tommy said they'd be. I turned the nose of my boat into the bank. The blade of my motor broke the ice and spun it away from her so I could back her around.

I didn't know them at that time, but Tommy and them hollered to each other by name. Their motor had lost its spark and wouldn't start. I towed them back across the Nanticoke and into Wapermander Creek. The water had already skimmed back over with ice, it was that cold. Tommy carried them on down where they'd left their pickup at Lewis Wharf.

***

Thank God nobody got hurt. That old T-Craft brought those guys through safely. The 200-horsepower Mercury was tough, too. One of my gunners was president of a cable company and they had that motor in a warehouse for testing cable. He took $2,500 off the asking price—practically gave it to me. I had ten members and guests aboard one day going down the Nanticoke to go ducking. We came up on two drift-netters with their workboat hung up on a big cake of ice. I slipped over there and broke them loose and we went on ducking.

***

– 208 –

Panic is what gets some in trouble, but some people will do anything for ducks. If they're not risking their lives, they're risking getting locked up. They tell a story down below about this local man who came in the store one day bragging.

He said, I got so many ducks today, I had to walk on the dead ones to get to the cripples.

A man standing by the counter said, You don't know who you're talking to.

No. Who?

I'm the federal game warden, said the man.

The hunter said, Well, you don't know who you're talking to.

Who?

I'm the biggest liar in Dorchester County.

***

One night back before I ever flew to Louisiana, I was sitting back all warm and nice watching television. Six or eight inches of snow lay on the ground outside. It had stopped coming down, but it was cold as iron.

Some boys from Seaford were gunning marsh above the Island, where they rented a little shanty from the Martineks. They'd been out there a couple days, but I didn't know anything about them till a knock came on the door. I got up and opened the door. There stood one of the gunners and a deputy sheriff. My first thought was, What have I done now?

I stepped back and said, Come on in out of the cold. What's goin' on?

The gunner said, Wylie, we need your help. I got my two buddies back at Martinek's shanty. They got wet and couldn't make it out, so I came out to get help. They got no heat left. A helicopter's coming from Patuxent, but we need somebody to go along to show 'em where the shanty's at.

I said, Can't you go? I never been up in the air.

He said, No, I don't think I can.

I said, I'm not too sure about it myself, but I'll go.

They'd already radioed the Naval Air Station for help. Wind was blowing a good twenty-five mile-an-hour, but a Navy pilot and co-pilot came on across Chesapeake Bay in a chopper and pitched her across the road from my house, those blades sending snow a-flying.

I climbed in the back seat, along with a state trooper.

The pilot asked me, Can you see all right back there?

I said, No, I need to see out both sides if I'm gonna spot that shanty.

He said, Come on up here with me.

The co-pilot climbed in back and I got up front with the pilot. He started the old blades whirling and we shot straight up in the air, sparks flying.

The pilot asked me, Which way?

I said, Southeast, about two miles.

He headed southeast and a couple miles out I saw something. From up there, it looked like a muskrat house— just a little dark speck in all that snow.

I pointed it out and said, That could be it over there. Check that out.

The pilot threw on this big spotlight and lit that shanty right up. He pitched down next to it and the trooper went inside and found those two guys half-froze. When the three gunners had used up all their fuel, they tried to come out on a high tide. Not knowing the marsh, these two got all wet falling in potholes, then they turned back to the shanty, while the third man who knew the marsh came out. They'd burned everything they could get their hands on, even Martinek's outhouse.

When they all climbed aboard, the pilot said, We're one person overloaded, but I think we can make it okay.

I didn't think too much of that, but he got things spinning and sparking and the old chopper finally lifted up.

They carried us to Cambridge Airport and left me there. I had to call the Island for a ride home.

***

When all the millionaires owned the clubhouses and marsh around here, they used to dump corn by the truckload. They kept the ducks healthy and fed to fly back and reproduce good. Come the next year, we had plenty of ducks. Now the government's buying up all the marsh and nobody dare feed a duck. Those nice clubhouses are left to fall down.

There were plenty of ducks in those old days, but not all that many deer. Just once in a while you'd see one. Driving back and forth to court Elliotts Island girls, me and my cousin Ted saw a few. Probably the first I ever killed was hitting a deer on one of those trips. When we came back in Daddy's new Buick, he looked in the trunk for something or other, and found a deer in there. Boy, he was saying something.

You boys gonna get in trouble. Here you got my trunk all bloody, he said.

Over the years, deer kept getting thicker. Later on I'd take parties out hunting. Herbert North, Sr. and Junior, came down to the Island one day bringing gunners from Baltimore. The guys wanted to go after deer. Herbert Senior told them he'd

Wylie in front of a group of visiting hunters

ask me to take them and brought them down to the house.

We got in their cars and went up to Axies Island, a

wooded spot in the marsh about four miles above Elliotts Island. We parked along the road, down below a turn.

One guy started into the woods and a fox ran out. He came running out after the fox and they all opened fire with 30.'06s, shooting up a storm. The fox lit off straight down the road. The guys started hollering and shooting hard as they could shoot, bullets ricocheting off the road around that fox.

Son-of-a-bitch, said one guy.

He pulled up a pants leg, and he had a red mark where he'd been grazed by a bullet.

I said, I'm through. Wrap it up; we're going.

And that's what we did. I wasn't going in the woods with them. They shot at anything that moved. If they didn't care about neither one of their own guys, I knew a bullet might hit me.

Chapter 35

ROCKFISHING

Old-time fishermen used to drive right through town with big rockfish and nobody blinked an eye. In my time, we had to deal with cows that came from an extra good spawn in the 1950s. When that crop hit up the Nanticoke River in the '70s and '80s, they cleaned out everything else. At first, nobody was used to seeing those big fish, 'cause they came overnight to spawn. Everybody except the fishermen got caught off-guard. The law didn't know that kind of fish was in there.

I usually had a guy called Gizmo with me. Normally we went out three to a boat and Gizmo went ashore on the marsh to clean fish. The third guy helped me run out the nets, right off from where Gizmo was fileting. Every time we made a drift, we went back to Gizmo and pulled the fish from the net. He cleaned the fish while we ran a net out again. We set a board on the marsh and a little light about three feet off the ground. You had to come right up on it to see it.

***

After midnight one night, two boats of us were fishing above the bridge in Vienna, Gizmo and another boy aboard with me in my boat, and the Duke and two guys with him. I laid my net out and the Duke laid his net out. When we started pulling ours back aboard, the net was full. In one drift, we caught nearly enough to sink our boat, the Duke did the same.

We hauled and hauled to get ours in the boat, till Gizmo was panting, I gotta quit. . .I gotta quit.

I said, No, you don't gotta quit. You gotta pull.

When we got the net in, the boat wasn't far out of the

water. We ran up into one of the little creeks to pull the fish out of the net, then me and Gizmo fileted out every one of them. The third guy scaled them with a hatchet. The Duke and his crew did the same. After we fileted out the meat, we hit the gut bag with the point of a knife and the fish carcass sank to the bottom of the creek. Then we got our boards and lights, loaded the filets aboard, and nobody could say we'd ever been there. We sailed on back down the river and, when we got to Vienna, the whole Methodist congregation was standing on the riverside watching us come in to the boat ramp. It was Easter morning and they were all there for sunrise service.

We had fileted out 1,140 pounds of meat, and I was back home in my bed before Easter Sunday got good and light. That's when I could afford to pay cash for my Chevrolet pickup, a Big-10 loaded with everything. Those big rock were coming in here destroying the small rock. What we did with those nets never hurt a thing—did good is what it did.

Shortly after that, the marine police went up that same creek on a low tide and their Whaler's motor choked out. Come to find out, they'd run up on a whole pile of carcasses.

***

Crab-potting down to the seaside one spring, I met a marine cop who used to work the Nanticoke when we were fishing.

He said, I used to get a feeling come over me when I saw your boat that something was wrong.

I had that same feeling myself one dark night when I'd loaded everybody's oversized fish on my boat. My truck was parked on a farm over in Wicomico County and I was running all our catch up a creek to unload. The Duke was in his boat in the river, watching the mouth of the creek to cover me. Getting up close to my truck, I got that feeling something's wrong. I saw a van backing a boat and trailer into the creek.

In the dark, it looked just like the tan police van with a Boston Whaler. I spun around and made a run for it, back out of the creek and down the river. When the boat came out behind me, the Duke started after it, but it turned away from me and went upriver.

Next day another fisherman said, The police were really thick on the river last night. When I put over in the creek, I ran up against two boats of 'em.

The Duke told me, Wylie, if that was the police, I wouldn't have let you get caught. I woudda run over 'em first.

And he probably would.

***

The Whalers' engines used to start a buzz in our CB radios when they got within a mile of us. We could tell from the hum how close they were getting. After they caught on and started monitoring us on our CBs, we fed them wrong information and ran them up and down the river. One cold, rainy night, we parked by the ramp in Vienna and sat in my truck talking on the CB watching them fly past this way and that.

When they finally came in, all cold and wet, one cop came over. I rolled down my window and he stuck his head in.

A fine lookin' crew, he said, *FINE LOOKIN' CREW*!

They didn't know how to catch nobody. They'd waste time and money putting a man undercover, then he'd blow his cover just to catch one old fella who caught a fish to eat for his supper.

***

I watched the DNR by the ramp in Vienna another day, their biologists turning loose a mess of hybrid rock. Before they hardly got the hybrids overboard, the seagulls had the fish. They were nice-looking, but the state raised them in shallow ponds. That's where those hybrids were used to swimming, so when they got in the river, they didn't want to get away from the top of the water. The seagulls fed up on all of them.

The agency always brought a camera along and the newspaper had pictures and articles about all these fish being stocked in the river. The biologists were just experimenting around. They said the hybrids couldn't spawn, so they couldn't harm the natural fish. For myself, I think the seagulls did us a favor eating up those hybrids.

***

In the late 1980s, the DNR barred us from fishing for rock altogether. They drove so many men off the water and

Wylie buying work gloves at Wheedleton's store in Galestown. Culling crabs, four pair might last a season, but culling oysters, a pair lasted only a couple days. Long trapping gloves cost $30 and got patched throughout the season.

out of work, there ain't nobody hardly out there fishing now. The year they closed it up, saying the fish were gone, there were plenty of fish. The last day of that season, before the moratorium came into effect, we caught 1,100 pounds on a couple drifts. The DNR likes to say the moratorium saved rock from near extinction, but rock were coming back in the natural cycle of things. Now they'll lose these rock we've got. They're gonna lose the whole works, 'cause the rock are gonna kill their own selves for lack of commercial men fishing.

One who's passed on is Elijah Wheedleton, who some called 'The Fish Doctor.' Elijah knew so much about fish, even one or two biologists had sense enough to listen to him. He caught a mess of fish in his days on the Nanticoke, before it was closed to us, and he sold many a one from his store in Galestown. We traded a lot up there.

***

When the state put all the fishermen out of work, they hired some to make owl boxes. Who the heck wanted more owls? The government's all for building up predators—owls, hawks, eagles, 'coons, foxes. Those predators already made more off my marsh than me.

The government is a predator itself, throwing nature out of whack with their regulations and experimenting. Jimmy found an injured eagle once near his house. He took his jacket off, walked up easy and quiet on this big thing, wrapped it up, and took it home. He called Blackwater Refuge, who sent a rescue team to take and nurse it. If some government agent had found that eagle instead of Jimmy, they would have sent a bunch of men and photographers out there carrying on— probably would have scared the thing to death.

Chapter 36

REGULATIONS

That time Jimmy saved the bald eagle and called the Refuge, the agency told newspapers that it probably had been caught in a pole trap and attacked by other predators. Jimmy didn't believe that. He said it had been attacked, all right, because of a cut down the side of its neck. There was no sign it ever got caught in any trap, though. He thought the government wouldn't admit it, but they'd loosed different predators at one time or another around Blackwater Refuge to control Sika deer. Sika's another species some agency turned loose here. All the nutria didn't come from fur dealers, either. Some escaped from an experiment the government ran, raising nutria on the Refuge.

Jimmy said there were mountain lions, wildcats, and wolverines over his way around the Refuge, too. He saw their tracks, and Jimmy knew his business. He couldn't keep up with his dogs well enough to see them, but they chased off after strange things all the time and came back cut up. The dogs brought back skeleton parts sometimes. He took one set over to Blackwater Refuge. The guy there wouldn't admit what it was, but he tried to keep the jaw bone. Jimmy wouldn't let him.

***

When they're not experimenting with different species, they're spraying chemicals to kill one thing or another. It would be okay if they just sprayed for mosquitoes on the Island, but they spray the whole marsh. The government never allowed aerial spray over their marsh on the Refuge and they had three-square grass growing so pretty and thick you had to burn it before you could walk. Coming around Fishing Bay toward the Island, where they sprayed pesticides, all you could see was waterbushes, mud, and phragmites.

***

The county and state spray other chemicals to kill weeds and phragmites while other agencies plant seedlings to bring back aquatic grasses. Then the tide and rain carry weedkiller overboard. I don't know who brought phragmites around here, but there never used to be any of that choking out the grasses ducks and geese feed on.

***

When I was winning the skinning contests at the Outdoor Show, I gave an earful to the city reporters who came to interview me. They didn't print the stuff about chemicals and how 'rats got tumors on their legs and bellies after the

---

THE WALL STREET JOURNAL   DOW JONES & COMPANY, INC.
Publishers
121 SOUTH BROAD STREET, PHILADELPHIA, PA 19107

March 18, 1982

Dear Wylie,

Well, you're famous now. Perhaps that means you can get a dollar or two more for your 'rats next year.

You made this story fun to do. Thanks for being so helpful. I hope next winter brings you better luck on the marsh. I'll be rooting for the critters to breed like crazy in the meantime.

Sincerely,

John Helyar

Letter from The Wall Street Journal *to* Wylie *after a front page article written about him was published.*

spraying started. The 'rats stopped breeding right, the ducks too, but when it came to the marsh, the newspapers just worried about animal rights and over-harvesting.

We used to get all kinds of people in the Nanticoke Inn. They'd walk in wearing leathers shoes and order a cheeseburger. After a couple beers, they wanted to argue about animal rights and the water.

I could tell them something about water pollution. Before all the chemicals, my one uncle had twenty-four kids he raised near a cannery that piped its waste overboard. Water black with tomato skins backed up in the ditch in front of his house. When you drove by his place, it looked like otters were swimming in the ditch. You'd see something duck through a pipe under the road, then heads would pop up out the other end, and it was those youngsters swimming around in there. They were the healthiest kids ever—never were sick a day and still aren't.

Now the government won't let you dump natural things like tomato skins overboard. Crab chum has to be trucked away inland. Chum's nothing but shell and guts from steamed crabs. Who got the bright idea that crab chum is bad for the water? It came out of the water, didn't it? It should go back. Tomato skins and chum would fertilize the bottom and grow grass.

Used to be, whenever you wanted a string of fish for your supper, you went down where the picking-house dumped chum to catch a mess of fish. If you put an eelpot there and didn't fish it out pretty quick, it was likely to burst. Now there's not enough for fish to eat, and nothing natural's fertilizing the bottom for grasses. All that stuff needs to be put back in the water, not in the landfill.

It should be a law, if your property's not waterfront, you should have to pack all that waste in a cannon and shoot it overboard.

***

I got no degree, but I can figure out what's going on. These experiments and regulations trying to change nature are just screwing everything up. Regulations are different from laws. Nobody votes these things in. Different agencies just fiddle about with them on their own, changing regulations nonstop. The way it used to be, there was always something a working man could turn to. If there weren't many rock, guys weren't making money rockfishing and just naturally went to something else. It all regulated itself. A man always had somewhere to turn to make a living, but they're taking that away from us with all the regulations. To make it on the water, you have to work all year. You can't make it doing just one or two things.

*C*hapter 37

RACCOONS, FROGS, AND BURGERS

A guy they called Master Baiter lived and trapped over in Wicomico County, but hung out in the Goat. Some bragging was going on in there one night about what a big 'coon was caught that day.

I said, You ain't caught no big 'coon. You should see the dumpster 'coons we're catching down home on Elliotts Island wharf.

Aw, you don't have no big 'coons down there like I caught.

I said, I got one weighed forty pounds. It's so big, after I skinned him out, I had to stretch his hide on an ironing board.

You ain't caught no forty pound 'coon.

Yes I have too, I said. You be up here tomorrow night. I'll bring him up here and show you.

In my garage freezer at home, I still had coyote and 'coon skins rolled up that the drifter had sent from Texas. I got one of those giant 'coons out to thaw. When I went up the road next day, I carried it into the Goat. The stretched hide spanned twice as wide as either table in there, so I rolled it out on the floor.

Jeez, said Master Baiter, where in the world did you catch that?

That's a Elliotts Island dumpster 'coon, I said. I caught him on the wharf.

Master Baiter's eyes were popping and he said, Wait till I call Dave.

He got on the payphone to Dave, a fur buyer in

Wicomico County, telling him about Elliotts Island dumpster 'coons.

***

When nothing much was going on in the Goat, around midnight me and Ray Moore might take a notion to go bull frogging. Ray was from down below too. We went on foggy nights in the spring, before crabbing started. Light holds a frog unless you get real rowdy jumping around. We waded out into ponds with flashlights and onion bags, snatching frogs up with our hands. If we had to move a snake aside to get to a frog, we didn't mind. One night every frog in the world was doubled up mating We'd snatch for one and come up with two. We caught three hundred frogs that night and sold them to Kool Ice for a dollar apiece.

Frogs are just like eating a piece of chicken, only better. I bet Ray Moore and me been over every pond in Dorchester County after frogs.

***

Another night me and Ray had been out fishing. We tied up by the ramp there in Vienna around two o'clock in the morning. We saw something coming along with a funny gait.

I said, Ray, looks like a dog coming for us.

Well, it wasn't a dog, it was a baby in a diaper heading uptown. People didn't believe their eyes when me and Ray walked in the Goat with a baby in our arms. Nobody recognized who he was.

They started adding up babies around town and said, It's got to be one of these.

We called three or four, till we hit on this one guy.

When he answered, we asked, Where's your baby at?

He's in the bed, he said.

You sure he's in the bed?

Yeah, I'm sure.

But when he checked, that baby wasn't there. He'd

gotten out of the crib and walked up the street. If he'd taken a right turn on Race Street instead of a left, he'd have gone in the river.

***

The customers in the Goat didn't change much, but the place was forever changing hands. Some owners kept good food and others didn't. One of its off-times, I took my dog Leroy in there and ordered us hamburgers. When the food came, Leroy wouldn't eat his, so I didn't eat mine either. Later years, Frances Hunt cooked there and she knew her way around a kitchen. Before the old Goat closed up, Billy Dolby served the best hamburgers you could find anywhere.

Some like Billy wouldn't drink in their own bar, but one earlier owner came in around eleven in the morning and started on Pabst Blue Ribbon. Late afternoons, he switched to liquor. The boys used to stage mock fights just to get him going. Somebody like the Duke would give a wink to Gizmo and, next thing you knew, they were wrestling on the floor like they wanted to kill each other. They heaved me out the door in one battle.

That owner kept a table full of plants in the far corner from where the bar stood. Duke and Gizmo hit the floor one day, then decided to go for the plants. Trouble was, they'd gone down too close to the bar and had to roll clear across the room. They tumbled over and over, just about running out of gas. They gave the owner too much time. He beat them to the corner by a whisker and snatch the plant table out of harm's way.

With some of the actions I had in there, I don't know how I never got barred. Grant got himself barred from time to time. One thing I know about him: you didn't want to eat your soup around Grant without staying right there, 'cause he'd put something in it. I got him back, though, after he'd put stuff in my food.

A bunch of us were sitting around Vienna carrying on in front of Alton Hurley's house one day about noon and I said, Let's go to the Goat and get a bowl of soup.

Good idea, Grant said.

I slipped around to Frank's market and got a box of Ex-Lax and went across the road to the Goat and gave it to the bartender.

Here, I said. Warm a few doses of this up in Grant's soup.

Next day, Grant didn't show up to go to work. Dougie Eberspacher fished with him then.

I said, Dougie, you better call Grant and see where he's at. He's generally here by now.

Dougie said, Yeah, maybe I'll give him a call.

His wife Mary answered the phone and said Grant had an upset stomach. He finally showed up, white as a sheet.

***

A few years after that, we were playing cards one night upstairs. Grant looked puffed up and red-faced.

I said, Grant, you got something wrong with you.

He went home that night and Mary carried him to the hospital. The next day he died of a brain aneurysm. It looks like they could punch a hole and relieve an aneurysm somehow. I think they could have saved him. He worked construction at the time and had just been hit in the head by a crane's bucket.

I miss old Grant.

I could say, Grant, let's go south.

He'd say, Okay.

I'd say, How long will it take you to get ready?

He'd say, Come on by the house and get me.

I'd go by his place and he'd come out with a grocery bag full of clothes.

Chapter 38

ADDING IT ALL UP

I'll soon have fifty years on the job with my gunning club, so I guess I filled the bill when they were looking for a local guide. We've lost a lot of our members over the years, but they all had good times when they came down gunning at the Vienna Canvasback and 'Rat Club.

Looking around here, I never thought it would come to this limit working on the water. Earlier times, I could fish, I could oyster, I could crab, I could muskrat, and keep that big hunting lodge going. I didn't want for no money. I started in October and went oystering. I oystered up till around Christmas. It started getting cold then and January I went fishing. If it was warm enough not to freeze up, I went muskrating. That went on till March, the end of muskrating, then I went fishing again. That ran straight into crabbing.

The oyster situation is most worrisome. Whoever dreamed just thirty years ago that we wouldn't have an oyster to catch around Fishing Bay. I'd have called anybody who told me that a damn fool. When this water straightens up, we'll have oysters again, but I don't know how long it's gonna take. Even after the water's right, they need to turn about a hundred boats loose towing bagless drudges—something like they use dredging oysters, only without the bag that does the catching. It doesn't take many oysters spawning to get them started on a come-back, but they need clean shell to catch the seed. Bagless drudges will dig the old shell out of all the silt that's built up. Then the seed spat will catch.

Hurricane Isabel might have cleaned things up some,

coming through here in 2003. I know down in Texas and Louisiana, in some ways they liked a hurricane. When one comes ashore, the surge goes up in those rivers and bayous, flushing out old bacteria and stuff. Hurricanes do a lot of damage, but they help too. Isabel striking here could be part of the oysters coming back in some places in 2004.

The agencies can't take time to stop and watch them multiply naturally, they want to put Asian oysters in here. That's a mistake. Our natural oysters coming back down below ain't gonna die given a chance. There's no money in an agency doing nothing, though. These diseases that kill oysters came from agencies experimenting with foreign things in the first place. It's the same as the nutria from South America that plague the marsh. The watermen get blamed for over-harvesting, but all the oysters and muskrat that disappeared didn't leave here by tong or trap.

One of the biologists who wants to bring in Asian oysters said he's got a 'fair amount of confidence' that they won't damage our oysters. I don't have any at all. Asian oysters brought one of these diseases in here to this water.

***

Last time I worked my 26s, we were tonging to Oxford. Oysters were scarce most everywhere else, but thick up there. Everybody was trying to get a piece of them. My boat I had there was only 22-feet, four feet shorter than my tong shafts. Willie and Robert helped me to steady the tongs and dump the oysters on the culling board.

We were getting ribbed from the other boats, How many Abbotts does it take to work a pair of 26s?

The last day I worked there I said, I ain't workin' with nothin' longer than my boat. When they gotta be longer than my boat, I'm gonna put 'em on the bank.

***

The boat Daddy built me, *Miss Wendy*, got put on the

bank too, but not by me. I'd sold her. I used the T-Craft most of the time, 'cause I could put her on the trailer and take off when I had to. You can't do that with wooden workboats, and they take a lot of care. The guy I sold her to worked *Miss Wendy* a little while, then hauled her up on land and burned her up. If I knew he was gonna do that, I'd never have sold her. I could have fixed her up. The day she died, she still wore that patch inside of her that Daddy made down to Cobb Island in 1962. It never did leak.

***

Daddy was eighty or more when he built his last boat. She was about thirty feet and he built her for himself, then sold her to a man down Taylors Island. She sat across from the store there up in a field last time I saw her. I think they were supposed to be working on her, but I don't know what they done with her. You can't lay up wooden boats like that. She draws open and dries up.

Watermen don't last forever, either, any more than boats do. A boat or body only has so much hard work in it. Arthritis gets a lot of trappers, fishing traps from cold water and running wet in their skiff all winter. A man gets sweating walking, then gets aboard his skiff and gets cold. Daddy was eighty-four when he died. He walked across many a piece of marsh and he kept at it till he left here. But before he died, he got down to where he just fished a few traps he could set along the roadside. He had emphysema bad and, like he used to say, if you can't breathe you can't walk.

Somebody asked him how he was getting along and he said, I'm just sittin' around miserating, watchin' the other guy work.

A few years ago, in the mid-90s, me and Willie were crabbing together. He thought I was dogging it.

Willie said, Dad, you've got to start putting out a little more.

He thought I had something left in the tank, but I told him, Hell, I got it right wide open now. I'm runnin' in high gear.

***

I think a lot about a couple older guys who used to work with me. They neither one had sons they worked with like I did. Al Garcia, who gave me and Jimmy his little skiff that started us crabbing, he started from nothing himself. When he first came down home from the service, man, his wife felt jealous over him. She was so afraid another woman would look at him, she made him grow whiskers. Wearing whiskers downgraded you in those days.

They lived about a mile and a half from us, between us and Shorters Wharf. Beautiful fresh water flowed there and they had a pipe running into the spring where you could get clear, cold water anytime. The spring never froze up. It kept the whole community going when they didn't have running water. The health department wouldn't like that. It's capped off now, I imagine, but I know where it's at. The path to Robbins Landing led back into the woods from Al's house.

After Al couldn't go out on his own, his last years he moved to the Island and worked with me. His hands shook awful and he'd reach in that cull box, his hand working, and those crabs would eat him right up. I'd be working the line and hear him.

Oooo, damn, Al said, and I knew one had him.

***

Brice Hurley was another nice old guy who culled for me. He's the one who heard my boat explode while sitting in his outhouse. Brice could cull some oysters. We worked together around Fishing Bay. Then, when he was around seventy, me and Sammy took him with us tonging on Patuxent River around Broomes Island. He'd been on the water his whole life but never been over that way before.

Me and Brice drove from Elliotts Island to Hoopers Island every morning. We met Sammy there and the three of us sailed across the Bay. We caught our limit and sailed back to Hoopers Island, where we sold our oysters.

When Brice got on the boat to go to work, you never heard nothing out of him. The boat could be sinking and he wouldn't tell you about it. Coming home from Broomes Island one day, it got too rough and we had to turn around. Heading back west, I happened to look down to the floor. Water stood a foot deep into her. Brice was sitting right into it and never said a word.

Sammy said, I'm not afraid of going down. I'm with the Lord and He'll bear me up.

I said, Good. If we start going down, I'm gonna climb on your shoulders.

***

To make it working on the water, you've got to love it. My grandson Jason, Willie's boy, he's a real waterman. When he was four or five years old, he baited up his own trotline—carried it in a bucket with a couple window sashes on either end for weights. He floated a basket inside an inner tube he tied to himself, and waded neck-deep in the river behind my mother-in-law's. In place of a chock, he put the line over his shoulder. It's hard to believe, but he netted about a bushel of crabs going back and forth like that one day.

Now Jason's got his own workboat and we say the same of him as we always said of Jimmy. He can find crabs.

My son Cory crabs too, but his regular job is trapping on the nutria program. Willie and Robert are full-time watermen. Wendy's son Jonathan loves fishing.

***

Working on the water—once it gets in your blood— it sticks with you. I never got rich on the water, but it's not supposed to make you rich. If a man wants a load of money, he better leave the water and find a different job. We're just supposed to get by. That's all we've done for generations. We see a lot of ups and downs, but if we're left alone to do our job, we'll keep on getting by.

*E*pilogue

Wylie in 2004 with his kids Willie, Cory, Wendy and Robert.

*W*ylie Abbott's 65th Birthday at the new Nanticoke Inn, January 16, 2005

*Ron Harding, Eddie Majors, Bob Mollock,
Ray Moore &Robert Abbott with Wylie .*

Wylie Abbott, Jr. Wylie, Sr., Wendy Abbott White and Robert Abbott

Ray Moore, Richard Barnett. and Doug Eberspacher with Wylie

*W*ylie's Obituary as it appeared in local papers

Wylie Marvin Abbott, Sr. was stricken at his home on Elliott Island one week after celebrating his 65th birthday with a host of family and friends,. He passed away February 18, 2005 at Coastal Hospice at the Lake in Salisbury, Maryland.

Born January 16, 1940, the son of Winnie and Dorothy Robbins Abbott, Wylie grew up in Robbins, Maryland and received a public education there and at Crapo and South Dorchester High School. Since the late 1950s, he has made his home on Elliott Island. His working life centered on the water and marshes of Dorchester County, as waterman, wholesale and retail seafood dealer, trapper, and hunting guide. For 45 years, he was employed as the guide of the Vienna Canvasback and 'Rat Club. He participated in every National Outdoor Show from 1950 to 2004, winning five junior muskrat-skinning contests in the 1950s, then winning the title of World Champion Muskrat Skinner thirteen times between 1970 and 1993. He held three permanent trophies for winning three consecutive world titles and was saluted with a plaque for his participation by the National Outdoor Show Foundation in 2002. He competed in the Former Champions' division through 2004 and planned to do so again in 2005.

Wylie was called to active service many times in Company K, 115th Infantry of the Maryland National Guard. He was a charter member of the Elliott Island Volunteer Fire Company and held a variety of offices over the years. At the time of his death, he was the company Fire Policeman. In addition to this public service, he was called on as a private citizen in numerous hunting emergencies. Disregarding his own safety and using his knowledge of local conditions and terrain, he played a key role in rescuing numerous hunters stranded in extreme weather on local marshes and waterways.

Feature stories about Wylie's outdoor mastery appeared in many newspapers and magazines, perhaps most notably on the front page of the *Wall Street Journal*. He also appeared on "Scorchy's Corner" with Scorchy Tawes and assisted the film makers and was featured in the award-winning documentary "Miss Nora's Store" in 1988. He attended Bounds and Elliott United Methodist Churches.

Wylie leaves his wife and son, Teresa Whaley Abbott and Cory Abbott of Elliott; and sons and daughter Wylie Abbott, Jr. and his wife, Pamela, of Elliott; Wendy Abbott White and her husband Keith, of Laurel, Delaware; and Robert Abbott and his wife, Trenie, of Laurel, Delaware; grandchildren Jason Abbott, Kristin Abbott, Jennifer White and Jonathan White; and numerous nieces and nephews.

In addition to his parents, he was preceded in death by his wife, Louella Gray Abbott, who passed away March 28, 1998, by his granddaughter Janie Rebecca Abbott, and by his brothers, James W. Abbott and W. Douglas Abbott, and sister, Ann Jackson.

A funeral service will be held Tuesday at 11 a.m. at Thomas Funeral Home in Cambridge, with the Rev. A. Delmer Willey Jr. officiating. Internment will follow at Elliott United Methodist Churchyard. The family will receive friends Monday evening from 7 to 9 at the funeral home. Pallbearers will be Jason Abbott, William Whaley, Jr. J. Stephen Gray, Douglas Eberspacher, Harold Brittingham, Wayne Phillips, Thomas Obrecht, and Richard Barnett. Honorary bearers will be Chester Martinek, Howard Martinek, Ray Moore, and Edward Majors.

Memorial offerings may be made to Elliott United Methodist Church, Coastal Hospice at the Lake, or to the Elliott Island Volunteer Fire Company.

Delivered at Wylie's Funeral
By Harold Dean Brittingham

I've not been around much in a long time, thanks in part to my line of work. I'd learned the waterman trade a long time ago and many's the time I've wished I'd stayed with it. It would have kept me closer to some good people. There were six men who had a great influence on my "upbringing,": my Dad Vince Brittingham of course, Richard

Wylie and Jake

© Brice Stump

Taylor, Leonard Shorter, Jack Owens, Warren Smith, and Wylie Abbott. Each man contributed something special to me. Wylie, along with my Dad, taught me about the outdoors. With Wylie teaching me the most about working the water. For these reasons, I felt compelled to write this:

THE HIP BOOTS IN THE CORNER

A husband, a father and a friend
Of the like this land won't see again.

Of crabs and fish caught, ducks and
Geese shot and oysters shucked
From a shell,

There have been so many
That no one could ever tell.

Quick as a cat, strong as an ox,
Wise as an owl and wily as a fox.

"Ya gotta know your knots, ol' boy,
If you're gonna learn this trade."

His guidance and influence will
Certainly never fade.

Playing golf? Well, I don't think
He ever did a round.

He was a waterman, by God!
And about the best to be found!

Skin five muskrats in about a minute
It was a wonder to watch the way
That he did it.

He could really bring in the ducks,
With a kernel or two
And along with all this, had honorable
Mention in Wall Street Journal too.

Quick to help friends and neighbor
Was a great joy.

And he did it with strength and
Endurance that matched Ol' Leroy

You'll call him a husband, a father
And a friend, as you look to the sky

I'll also call him a legend
And legends never die!

Some others added:

Even as a child, Wylie was always the life of the party. The party started when Wylie got there.

***

The word No wasn't in Wylie's vocabulary. He was a soft touch for anyone who needed a loan. You could say, Wylie, you're never gonna get that money back. He'd say, That's okay, they need it worse than I do.

***

He never saw the glass as half-empty.

Some of Wylie Abbott's duck hunting friends had this to say about him.

. . . We had some wonderful years of hunting together, a few parties, and a lot of laughs. We will all miss him. He was a real "Waterman" in the truest meaning of the word.

***

. . . Wylie showed us so many wonderful times duck shooting on the Nanticoke, tonging for oysters, having his dogs retrieve his penknife in the marsh near the old clubhouse, and guiding his boat at high speed through the marshes that I believed he was indestructible. I will never be able to think about Elliotts Island and all that marsh country without his wonderful spirit being part of it.

***

I will miss his great stories about the past and the wonderful times we had together. When I think of Wylie, he reminds me of one of the last pioneers of the century. His love of the marsh, hunting ducks, fish, and trapping for a living really inspired all of us to appreciate the true beauty of the place we call Elliott Island.

***

Wylie was a true through the core Eastern Shoreman. A rare and genuine individual, he represents all that is good about that very special part of the world. I always loved watching him on the water driving the boat to the blind in the worst of weather. He was so rugged, and to watch him skin a 'rat was just amazing to me. He was a unique person and I am certain that there will never be another quite like him. It was my good fortune to have known him.

A.M. Foley and Patrick J. Lynch

ABOUT THE AUTHOR

A. M. Foley has written numerous articles for regional and national publications and co-authored a history of her adopted home, *Elliott's Island: The Land That Time Forgot* with Freddie T. Waller, and two local pictorials, *Cambridge* and *Dorchester County,* with Gloria Johnson. Ann's first published fiction will appear in 2006 in the anthology *Mules, Motorcycles, and Memories.*

She has made her home on Elliott Island since 1977.